Bridging the Progressive-Traditional Divide in Education Reform

This book brings together a variety of connected voices which consider potential ways forward for school reform. By demonstrating how the 'subject-centered' and 'student-centered' models of education can, and have been working together in various contexts, the text sets out a compelling case for an emerging movement that unites ideologies and pedagogical traditions which have traditionally been considered to be at odds with one another.

In drawing from historical sources, the full range of contemporary research, and a series of investigations led by the authors, this book documents the deep back-story of school reform, and explains the powerful and largely unacknowledged consensus on what constitutes excellence in teaching and learning.

This book will be of great interest to researchers, academics, and postgraduate students in the fields of school reform and educational leadership. It will also appeal to graduate students, researchers and postgraduates in the fields of history of education, educational leadership, teaching and learning, and curriculum studies.

James Nehring is an associate professor of Educational Leadership in the College of Education at the University of Massachusetts Lowell, U.S.A.

Stacy Szczesiul is an associate professor of Educational Leadership in the College of Education at the University of Massachusetts Lowell, U.S.A.

Megin Charner-Laird is an associate professor in the School of Education at Salem State University, U.S.A.

Bridging the Progressive-Traditional Divide in Education Reform

A Unifying Vision for Teaching, Learning, and System Level Supports

James Nehring, Stacy Szczesiul, and Megin Charner-Laird

Routledge
Taylor & Francis Group

New York London

First published 2019
by Routledge
605 Third Avenue, New York, NY 10017

and by Routledge
2 Park Square, Milton Park, Abingdon, Oxon, OX14 4RN

First issued in paperback 2020

Routledge is an imprint of the Taylor & Francis Group, an informa business

© 2019 Taylor & Francis

The right of James Nehring, Stacy Szczesiul, and Megin Charner-Laird to be identified as authors of this work has been asserted by them in accordance with sections 77 and 78 of the Copyright, Designs and Patents Act 1988.

Library of Congress Cataloging-in-Publication Data
Names: Nehring, James, author. | Szczesiul, Stacy, author. | Charner-Laird, Megin, author.
Title: Bridging the progressive-traditional divide in education reform : a unifying vision for teaching, learning, and system level supports / James Nehring, Stacy Szczesiul and Megin Charner-Laird.
Description: New York, NY: Routledge, [2019]
Identifiers: LCCN 2019014615 (print) | LCCN 2019021807 (ebook) | ISBN 9780429424700 (E-book) | ISBN 9781138354616 (hardback)
Subjects: LCSH: Educational change—United States. | Education—Aims and objectives—United States. | Competency-based education—United States. | Progressive education—United States. | Motivation in education—United States. | Children with social disabilities—Education—United States.
Classification: LCC LA217.2 (ebook) | LCC LA217.2 .N44 2019 (print) | DDC 370.11—dc23
LC record available at https://lccn.loc.gov/2019014615

ISBN 13: 978-0-367-72804-5 (pbk)
ISBN 13: 978-1-138-35461-6 (hbk)

Typeset in Times New Roman
by Apex CoVantage, LLC

Contents

Acknowledgements

We are grateful to the copyright holders of several previously published works, of which we are the authors, for permission to use the material in adapted form in this book. The previously published works are as follows:

Nehring, J., Charner-Laird, M. and Szczesiul, S. (2019, February 16) Redefining excellence: Teaching in transition, from test performance to 21st century skills. *NASSP Bulletin*, 1–27. DOI: 10.1177/0192636519830772.

Nehring, J., Charner-Laird, M. and Szczesiul, S. (2017). What real high performance looks like. *Phi Delta Kappan, 98* (7), 38–42. DOI: 10.1177/0031721717702630.

Nehring, J., & Szczesiul, S. (2015). Redefining high performance in Northern Ireland: Deeper learning and 21st century skills meet high stakes accountability. *Journal of Educational Change, 16* (3), 327–348. DOI: 10.1007/s10833-015-9250-8.

Nehring, J. (2011). Are we headed in the wrong direction? *Phi Delta Kappan, 93* (2), 80.

Nehring, J. (2009) *The Practice of School Reform: Lessons from two centuries.* SUNY Press.

We are grateful to the United States Department of State for a Fulbright award that enabled much of the work supporting this book. We are grateful also to the Provost's Office of the University of Massachusetts Lowell for a seed grant, and the Center for Irish Partnerships at UMass Lowell for a mini-grant. In addition, we wish to thank The Senator George J. Mitchell Institute for Global Peace, Security and Justice, at Queens University Belfast for supporting our work.

We would like to acknowledge the contribution of several colleagues who participated in the development of the theoretical framework that launched the series of studies on which this book is based. They are Rivka Eisikovits,

Lily Orland-Barak, and Merav Ben-Nun from the Faculty of Education of the University of Haifa; also Martin Hagan and Frank Hennessey from the Department of Educational Studies, St. Mary's University College, Queens University Belfast.

We are also grateful to the approximately 420 participants in the studies that form the foundation for this book. Teachers, students, and school leaders welcomed us and gave generously of their time. Our thanks go also to Tony Szczesiul for expert editorial support.

Introduction
Non-Honors English

*Standing at the front of the classroom, Marie Hilliard said to her students,
"Fear can be a positive force, motivating people to follow a moral path."
Then she waited.*

*It was a gray, foggy day. Morning traffic crawled on the street below. . . .
Sleep was on the minds of many of the tenth graders in Marie's 'non-honors'
English class, but they slowly left their seats and spread out around the room.
Soon, several were standing at each of the room's four corners, depending on
whether they 'strongly agreed,' 'agreed,' 'disagreed,' or 'strongly disagreed.'
They started to look more awake.*

*It was the back half of October, and they'd been reading Chinua Achebe's
classic novel,* Things Fall Apart, *about the Igbo people of Nigeria, when
British colonials were beginning to sweep away Igbo culture. The main
character is Okonkwo, a young warrior.*

With further prompting from Marie, students began to speak up.

*Thomas, a lanky 15-year-old, said, "Fear of hell doesn't make you do
something because it's morally good—because in your heart you think it's
good. You're doing it because you're scared."*

*Alan, right next to Thomas, wearing a yellow ski vest said, "Yeah, if
you're getting someone to follow a path because of fear, that's not really a
positive, that's a negative because you're scaring them into doing what they
should do." The two boys looked at each other and nodded.*

*From the other side of the room, the 'strongly agree' corner, Lori Ann
spoke up. "Fear sharpens your senses. Okonkwo changed to be more hard
working; he had fear of being like his Dad."*

*Janet, in the 'disagree' corner, replied. "Fear makes you do crazy things.
He ended up beating his son because he was acting lazy, but he is just a boy
and that's what boys do, act lazy." The room tensed at Janet's remark.*

*Marie, the teacher, added quickly, with a smile, "people in general." And
everyone seemed to relax.*

*The students, fully engaged now, continued to mix it up for another min-
ute and then Marie said, "Okay, next prompt. Please move to the corner of*

your choice for this one: 'One's reputation is an easy thing to lose and a hard thing to replace.'" The class grew quiet, and then, in a single burst of energy, moved to their places, eager to pick up the conversation.[1]

Another day in an American high school. The kind of lesson you might see in a thousand classrooms, as the great engine of public education does its daily work. Interesting, but not really exciting. Right?

Actually, if this small scene *were* somehow typical—just another day, see it in a thousand classrooms—the news cycle would not churn with endless headlines about the need for school reform. That's because, if you look closely at what's happening in this classroom, and where it's happening, you *should* get excited, *very* excited. We did.

We spent several years visiting schools and classrooms,[2] mostly in urban neighborhoods serving families with little money and marginal health care. Mostly people of color, many students were recent immigrants learning English. Some had learning disabilities. Others were emotionally scarred by childhood trauma. All had strengths, diverse talents, deep funds of knowledge from their life experiences, and enormous potential to learn. The education lingo for neighborhoods like this is 'high need.' High need students now make up more than half of all students in U.S. public schools.[3]

What's striking about Marie's class is not the strategies and techniques she used, though they were very good. It's also not the sequencing of activities, though they were logical. What's striking about Marie's class is the intellectual demand she made of her students and the engagement by her students in the work. What's also striking is the skill with which Marie directed the class. Like when Janet said, "and he is just a boy and that's what boys do, act lazy." Marie knew that tag-comment about boys was likely to incite the boys in class, and, even as Janet was saying it, Marie felt the temperature in the room rise. So, without missing a beat, literally, without missing the one second beat of time it would take for the discussion to go off the rails, Marie said, "people in general," with a tone and a gesture to the class that said, *we know it's not just boys so please don't be distracted by Janet's targeting of boys.* It also said to Janet, *Be aware of your audience. If you want the boys in the room to listen, don't insult them.* It also said to the whole class, *See, I am looking out for you. As your teacher, I will allow us to explore freely, but I will keep the conversation emotionally safe for everyone.* It was a small moment, a tiny intervention, but it kept a fragile, important conversation moving in a positive direction and it provided instruction, differentiated to the needs of various class members. And it constituted a choice. Marie could have taken the discussion in several directions. She could have used Janet's offhand remark as the starting point of a conversation about gender, as portrayed in the book, as lived among the students in class. She could have used it to explore the nature of civil debate. Or she could set it aside, as she did, maybe for later, in order to maintain the current topic. The work of an alert and capable teacher shows in these smallest of moments, and the cumulative effect is a class with deep intellectual demand, deep student engagement, and the kind of learning that pundits tell us we need for "the 21st century" even though it's what our schools should have been teaching all along.

What's also striking about Marie's class is that at the same moment her students were engaged and learning, many of the classrooms in the rest of the school were not so alive, which, unfortunately, is common in American public high schools. In math class, students went through the motions of a problem set, with the teacher stepping them through procedures. In history class, students copied notes from the board about the causes of the American War of Independence. And so on. The differences might be lost on a casual observer, but the differences are there—subtle and deep—and they matter.

The question to ask is how do we make every classroom, especially those with students from historically-marginalized groups, as intellectually alive as Marie's? It's the question this book takes on. The answers may surprise you. We can tell you right now what the answer is *not*. It's not that we need more 'progressive' schools or that we need more 'traditional' schools. That's because good teachers and good schools blend the best of both. The answer is not that we need to 'get tough,' whether our toughness is directed against teachers or schools or students. And the answer is not more testing.

We argue, in this book, that the answer is right in front of us. It's Marie, and other really good teachers, and what they do every day. The solution is simple, but it's also painfully elusive.

Notes

1. All student quotes are verbatim from an audio-recorded classroom observation. Order has been changed and descriptive details added for readability. Pseudonyms are used.
2. "We" and "our" are used throughout the book to refer to the studies led, collectively, by the authors, though some studies included just one or two of us.
3. Suitts, S., Barba, P., & Dunn, K. (2015). *A New Majority: Low Income Students Now a Majority in the Nation's Public Schools*. Atlanta, GA: Southern Education Foundation. www.southerneducation.org/. This study reports findings from the National Center for Education Statistics, which are based on eligibility for the Federal Free and Reduced Lunch program. It does not account for English-language learners or students with special needs. Doing so would increase the majority of high-need students.

Part I

A Unifying Vision for Teaching and Learning

1 Exemplary Teaching and the Unacknowledged Consensus

What skills do you need to be a successful adult? It turns out there are roughly 25, if you review the relevant literature.[1] Which of these skills do schools regularly teach? Just three. That's what we found in nine of the highest-rated secondary schools in Massachusetts.[2]

Although we've known for decades, based on research, that classrooms tend to focus on lower-level cognitive skills—application, recall, and analysis—we were shocked to find in a series of studies in public secondary schools, that this pattern remains so strong, even in schools considered among the very best. But we also discovered that a significant minority of excellent teachers taught nearly the full range of skills and that their classes spanned subjects, grade levels, and academic tracks. We believe the system can learn a great deal from what these teachers do in their classrooms every day.

We also believe, based on themes from the literature framing our studies, that there is strong agreement in policy, research, and pedagogy backing what these teachers do—but the agreement is largely *unrecognized*. The more we read, the clearer it became. First, we examined large-scale research studies and policy reports, and found they affirmed the practices we observed. Then we looked at two great pedagogical lineages, commonly called "traditional" and "progressive," and found elements of both in the daily practice of the teachers, demonstrating that a centuries-old rivalry is entirely unnecessary. We also saw these same teachers enacting emerging pedagogies that promote positive identity formation, often with students representing groups historically marginalized.

It turns out there is a powerful, unacknowledged consensus about what constitutes good teaching. We wondered why it's not reaching into schools and creating a new norm for public education. To answer this question, we looked at the history of teacher practice, key education policies in the United States, and the socio-political forces that have shaped them. We also asked what can be done, within the education sector, at all levels, to counter negative forces and advance this powerful, widely-endorsed vision.

Bridging the Progressive-Traditional Divide makes the case that many actors across the fields of research, practice, and, to a growing extent, policy, are working in parallel, sometimes unaware of each other's efforts. Independently, they are building the basis of a new consensus that dissolves old ideological battle lines and may reduce historic inequities. We intend to propel this vision toward a broad social movement by telling its largely untold story and recommending actions in policy and practice.

What Great Teachers Do

In 2009, two of this book's authors (Nehring and Szczesiul) began a collaboration with several education researchers from the United Kingdom and Israel-Palestine. We were interested in policy literature from provincial and national systems, including our own, that claimed to advance a broad range of skills required for a global economy and a culturally diverse society, frequently called "21st century." We were interested because the same systems relied heavily on large-scale tests to measure learning, even though an abundance of research showed that such tests tended to limit what gets taught in schools, particularly schools serving disadvantaged communities where test pressure bears down hard. How ironic, we reflected, that education systems incentivized a very limited approach to teaching, while advocating for very expansive "21st century skills." Because test scores were the main accountability metric, all those broader and deeper skills, though vaunted in the promotional literature, appeared, from the research, to be largely absent in practice.

A study began to take shape. What if we could find schools serving high needs communities that not only performed well on the state exams but *also* showed evidence of teaching those deeper and broader capabilities? If such outlier schools existed, they could teach us all a great deal. What resulted was a series of five investigations over a period of eight years involving 24 secondary schools in the United States and the United Kingdom.[3] We interviewed teachers, principals, and students, sat in on professional meetings, visited classes, and collected instructional documents. A total of 420 teachers, students, and administrators participated directly in the set of studies.[4] Altogether, the five investigations produced a wealth of information about teaching and schools.

Our first challenge was to clarify the murky "21st century skills" construct. By sheer luck, that massive task had recently been accomplished for us by an august research organization. In 2010, the National Research Council (NRC) was getting started with a new project that held the potential to re-shape education policy. Recent decades had witnessed a growing chorus of interest groups and academics lamenting the inability of new employees to engage in crucial work-related tasks such as collaboration, problem solving, and communication. They lamented, also, the increasing failure of employees to show personal qualities such as persistence, time management, reflection, and self-awareness. In reports and studies, these skills and attributes were given various names, such as "next generation skills," "college and career readiness," "the new basics," "critical thinking," and "21st century skills." There seemed to be some common themes, but no clarity. The NRC set out to define the ideas behind such terms, clarify what existing research could tell us about them, and, by extension, potentially set a new agenda for public education.[5] The NRC team began by teasing apart the ideas behind various overlapping terms. Under the guidance of program officer Margaret Hilton, the steering committee began an extensive consultation with experts and a review of literature in psychology and economics. The effort came to fruition in 2012 with the publication of a substantial volume co-edited by James Pellegrino and Margaret Hilton, *Education for Work and Life: Developing Transferable Knowledge and Skills in the 21st Century*.[6]

The report took a broad view arguing for a public education focused on preparation for work, citizenship, parenting, and personal fulfillment. It fostered a sense of urgency by invoking the need for workers with more sophisticated skills required by a technology-driven workplace, and the pressing need to solve environmental and social problems. They identified three broad categories of competency required for an education up to the challenge: cognitive, intrapersonal, and interpersonal. The report described them as follows:

- The Cognitive Domain includes three clusters of competencies: cognitive processes and strategies; knowledge; and creativity. These clusters include competencies such as critical thinking, information literacy, reasoning and argumentation, and innovation.
- The Intrapersonal Domain includes three clusters of competencies: intellectual openness; work ethic and conscientiousness; and positive core self-evaluation. These clusters include competencies such as flexibility, initiative, appreciation for diversity, and metacognition (the ability to reflect on one's own learning and make adjustments accordingly).
- The Interpersonal Domain includes two clusters of competencies: teamwork and collaboration; and leadership. These clusters include competencies such as communication, collaboration, responsibility, and conflict resolution.[7]

In addition to "competencies," the NRC report emphasized the importance of transfer, "the process through which an individual becomes capable of taking what was learned in one situation and applying it to new situations" (p. 5).[8] Consistent with research on transfer, the report acknowledged that the teaching of domain-specific knowledge (i.e., "subjects") is necessary to anchor competencies. That is to say, it is not effective to teach students to think critically without providing something to think critically about. Instruction must build disciplinary knowledge while also building competency across all three domains—cognitive, intrapersonal, and interpersonal. The message was clear: teach "the basics" interwoven with "21st century skills" in order to achieve what the National Research Council called "deeper learning."

We now had clarity about what we should look for. The next challenge was how to measure it. There are currently no reliable and readily accessible metrics for some of the skills included in the NRC taxonomy, such as collaboration and teamwork, conflict resolution, responsibility, and flexibility. How could we ever document the degree to which students were learning these skills and make comparisons across classrooms and schools? We couldn't. But what we could do was measure the instructional demand for these skills. A line of scholarship going back to Walter Doyle in the 1980s has investigated the nature of knowledge and skills required by instructional tasks.[9] While we could not measure whether students were learning various complex skills, we could measure whether the tasks to which students were directed required them. And we knew from work done by Richard Elmore that the tasks required of students powerfully shape their learning, summarized in Elmore's compact phrase, *Task predicts performance*: "What determines what students know and are able to do is not what the curriculum says they are supposed to do, or even what the teacher thinks he or she is asking students to do. What predicts performance is *what students are actually doing*. The single biggest observational discipline . . . is to look on top of the desk, rather than at the teacher in front of the room."[10] Instructional demand would become our proxy for student learning.

Taxonomy in hand, we set out to find which of these skills get taught in schools. We decided to look at secondary schools serving high-need communities in our home state, Massachusetts, focusing, in particular, on those that reliably produced comparatively high scores on state tests. According to system measures, which put a laser-like focus on test outcomes, these would be the best schools. And because Massachusetts regularly ranks high in national and international comparisons, these schools would be—according to the system—the best of the best.

As a first step, we invited all teachers in nine high-performing schools to submit instructional materials from a single week. We received 155 instructional items (classroom worksheets, homework assignments, project descriptions, rubrics, quizzes, tests, and so on) from 73 classrooms. Analyzing the nearly 2,000 instructional tasks embedded in these materials, we found that recall-and-application topped the list, with analysis a distant third and only occasional demands for evaluation and creative thinking—altogether a grim finding. The picture became more disturbing when we looked at the inter-personal and intrapersonal domains—at skills like communication and trust building, or adaptability and self-regulation—where task demand for a student in any of these top-performing schools was either rare or wholly absent from a full week of classroom instruction.

To better understand the dynamics behind these concerning patterns, we decided to take a deeper dive, with a second study in which we looked more closely at three schools that appeared to have a pronounced focus on deeper learning. We observed 22 classrooms, interviewed school leaders, and spoke with teachers in focus groups. Classroom observations, which were audio recorded and meticulously scrutinized, revealed more of the same—that is, for most classes, an instructional focus on recall, application, and, occasionally, analysis, with every other skill listed in our taxonomy either rarely addressed or wholly absent. Why, we asked, did schools that talked a good line about 21st century skills continue to not teach them?

In focus groups, teachers often referred to higher-level thinking, critical thinking, or 21st century skills; in class, they often said to students, "I'm pushing you here," "I'm demanding more now." There was clearly plenty of *talk* about academic demand, but what was the nature of the demand *in classrooms*? To that end, we looked closely at tasks assigned to students. Comparing all classes where greater intellectual demand appeared to be on the mind of the teacher, we found that it took three forms, which we called "more stuff," "more steps," and "deeper learning." Only one of these, as the names imply, fostered learning of skills across our taxonomy.

More Stuff

In some classes, teachers presented students with complex content. How-ever, the tasks assigned to students did not require complex thought. Although the content was complex, the tasks were simple, mostly requiring no deeper skills than recall or application. This was apparent, for example, in an Advanced Placement U.S. government class for 11th and 12th graders. On the day we observed, the teacher was reviewing material from a text-book chapter. The lesson consisted mainly of the teacher stating terms, ask-ing students recall-level questions about definitions and asking questions that called on students to apply the terms. To be successful in this class, students needed to be familiar with a number of terms, such as 'demograph-ics,' 'party identification,' 'Democrat,' 'Republican,' 'blue state,' 'red state,' and 'purple state.' They also had to be able to apply the terms to simple problems—for example, naming factors that predicted a person's party affiliation. Although the required vocabulary appeared to grow daily and was quite extensive, no deeper learning demands were made of the students during this lesson. While the content was highly relevant to the discipline of political science, any conceptual understanding rooted in the discipline was absent. It was just content. It was just *more stuff.*

More Steps

In other classes we observed, the teacher assigned tasks that required complex directions and procedures but little complex thought. In an elective History class for 11th and 12th graders, for example, the teacher was transitioning students to the next chapter in a textbook. Delivering the content at a blistering pace, the teacher gave a series of directions that referred to chapter classifications, videos, articles, learning objectives, learning targets, learning outcomes, an essential question, a guiding question, a project, online quizzes, self-pacing, corrections, and a required 100% on all quizzes. A student paying close attention would find the number and complexity of these steps daunting. (We did.) But when the class turned to reviewing the studied material, task demand was strictly at the recall level. Here's a short excerpt:

TEACHER: Why is the solar system or the Earth considered a new threshold? So who can tell me basically what makes it a threshold? You need to identify the ingredients and the conditions. What are the ingredients? What did you have?

STUDENT: Dying stars.

TEACHER: Dying stars. No one can give that answer again. And you need to have clouds of?

STUDENT: Gas.

TEACHER: Clouds of gas and dust and matter. So we talked about clouds of matter and newly forming stars and dying stars which gives us what? What do we need?

STUDENT: Chemicals.

TEACHER: The chemistry, the chemicals, right?

Teacher questions here were strictly recall of material covered in the chapter. Comprehension was not even required for some questions when, for example, the teacher provided part of a technical phrase ("clouds of___") and the student needed only to fill in the blank by parroting the correct word ("gas").

In this class and others like it, the teacher made some complicated demands of her students, but the demands, purely procedural, led nowhere.

They did not foster deeper disciplinary knowledge, nor did they scaffold instruction toward greater cognitive, interpersonal, or intrapersonal demand. It was just a lot of complicated procedures, maybe like those that a health insurance claim often involves, that does not produce a reimbursement. It was procedures that led nowhere—*more steps.*

Because we did not conduct follow-up interviews with the observed teachers, we cannot know how they would explain the gap between their claims about teaching 21st century skills and the reality of the instruction we observed. That was a limitation of our study. We could, however, rule out some possibilities. Because no association was observed between grade level, academic subject (including tested and non-tested subjects), academic track, and instructional demand, we can be reasonably confident that, in these schools at least, they were not major factors. That suggests the reasons may be more idiosyncratic, having to do, perhaps with teacher beliefs. Here's where we turn from the UMass Lowell study to a wealth of contemporary research on teacher beliefs. Teacher epistemic beliefs, according to a large body of research, influence how a teacher conceives and enacts instruction for deeper learning. In particular, teacher beliefs about the nature of knowledge play a major role, and they vary widely. There is abundant research demonstrating this fact, particularly when it comes to teacher beliefs about the nature of knowledge within their own academic disciplines.[11]

Within many academic disciplines, beliefs about the nature of disciplinary knowledge range widely. Researchers have derived elaborate schema to represent this variety. Comparing schema, a broad pattern is discernible. Though a simplification, it is nonetheless useful to summarize the range of teacher epistemic beliefs as a continuum. At one end, knowledge is seen as certain and fixed, at the other, knowledge is tentative and socially constructed. It is only a small leap to infer that pedagogy associated with the former will tend toward transmission of information with memorization of facts and formulas, while pedagogy associated with the latter will tend toward inquiry, collaboration, and problem solving. This inference is supported by research demonstrating that teacher beliefs powerfully influence instruction.[12] While research suggests a strong link between teacher epistemic beliefs and instruction, it also suggests the influence is not linear.

Among the 22 classrooms we observed, the majority displayed an earnest but misguided understanding of deeper learning. 15 of the classrooms showed some combination of content-heavy teaching ("more stuff") or procedurally dense teaching ("more steps"). These were disheartening findings; however, fully seven of the classrooms, roughly a third in our sample, showed us something entirely different. Findings from the other studies in our series of studies in the U.S. and U.K. supported these patterns.

Deeper Learning

We turn now to an example of a class in which teaching for deeper learning is abundant. It is both inspiring and representative of the teachers we observed who teach for deeper learning. We follow the example with a discussion of themes that emerged across classrooms where deeper learning was in evidence.

The example is a Humanities class for students in grades 11 and 12, a non-honors track in a tracked school serving a high poverty, urban community. Students were beginning a new unit. Having just completed a unit on Western imperialism in Africa, they were turning to a study of Western imperialism in China. Students were tasked with inventing questions to guide their study. The teacher led students through brainstorming possible questions based on what they wondered about China at that time, then asked them to narrow their list of questions based on what they felt was most important, and then helped them shape their questions to ensure they were intellectually stimulating and open-ended. Students asked, for example, "Why did countries want to imperialize China?" "How did they [the Chinese] succumb to imperialism?" "How was Chinese culture disrupted [due to imperialism]?" The exercise developed analytical and evaluative skills. Additionally, the collaborative way that students generated their questions, coached by their teacher, fostered interpersonal skills (communication, cooperation, negotiation, assertiveness, and advocacy). Moreover, the norms that this teacher enforced throughout the individual, small group, and whole class activities fostered intrapersonal skills such as self-monitoring and self-evaluation. In this class and others like it, student tasks ranged across all three domains of our taxonomy.

This classroom example highlights the depth and breadth of intellectual demand that defines deeper learning. With some further analysis, it also shows us what the teacher did to create conditions in the classroom that fostered deeper learning. In this instance, the complexity of decision making and situational awareness displayed by the teacher was, frankly, astonishing. Here is an excerpt of just four minutes of instruction, using a two-column format to capture the moves made by the teacher in the left column (transcript with descriptive details) and commentary in the right column (Table 1.1). It was the Monday after Thanksgiving vacation. The transcript starts at the beginning of class just as students were nearly all seated. We recommend reading the entire left column first to see what happened and then read the entire right column for commentary.

The lesson that followed this short segment gestured back to the previous unit (a study of Africa) and introduced the new unit (a study of China) as described above. The rear-looking gesture was the return of a set of essays,

Table 1.1 Decision Making and Situational Awareness During Four Minutes of Instruction

Time (minutes)	Transcript with descriptive details	Commentary
0:00	*T. leading an informal conversation about what people had for Thanksgiving dinner.* S1. And for Christmas we're gonna make the same thing. S2. Yeah. I know. We had the same exact thing. T. Well, you know, you guys could follow Jeremiah's lead. He made his own meal so you know what? I think this should be your challenge. You guys could make your own meal and you know I think you should, for Christmas, you guys volunteer to make dinner for your families and you make what you want to make.	Students are complaining about how their Thanksgiving family dinners were boring, all the same stuff as every other year. Teacher picks up on one student who did his own cooking. She affirms that student's initiative and suggests, as a reply to the complaining students, that they do likewise. Her tone is light (there's plenty of laughter throughout the exchange) but pointed. She seizes this moment as a way to connect with her students while also teaching a small lesson in empowerment: if you don't like the way someone else is doing something, then step up to do it yourself.
1:49	*The Thanksgiving dinner conversation continues with the teacher sharing what she made and explaining how people in her house made the meal together. Students and teacher share favorite dishes.*	Teacher is allowing the conversation to continue, though it appears the time for class has begun. By allowing it, she is expressing value in this conversation as a way to connect with students, affirming a topic that is of interest to them, demonstrating that it is of interest to her too; thus, they have a shared personal interest, a basis for a relationship. She also uses the opportunity to model cooperative meal-making as a further answer to the students' earlier complaint about having the same thing every year.
1:43	*Next, the teacher attempts to redirect the class from the Thanksgiving conversation to the planned lesson.* T. Alright. So welcome back. guys. Now that we've debriefed our lovely Thanksgiving in which [student name] got home to have her Mom's lovely mac and cheese so she was happy [inaudible student talk and laughter] S. She cooked it mostly before I got there. T. Oh. Okay. [Pause.] So she could spend more time with you. S. Yeah. T. Aww. There you go.	The teacher transitions, warmly, with a "welcome back" statement and a parting nod to the Thanksgiving conversation (the "lovely mac and cheese"). Her parting nod, however prompts further talk about Thanksgiving. She acknowledges this talk even though it is in direct opposition to her attempt to transition to the day's lesson because, apparently, it touches on a sensitive mother–daughter relationship. By allowing it, she demonstrates to the students that she is a teacher who balances student emotional needs with curriculum.

(Continued)

Table 1.1 (Continued)

2:15	Alright. Okay you guys. So here's what I want to do today. And I know your Do Now asks you to compare it to the movie that we did end up watching because we had just a few people on Friday. So what I'd like you guys to do is on this Venn diagram, would you please put down just preliminary thoughts? What do you know about Chinese culture? You know, list what you know about American culture, and in the middle any similarities that you think exist between these two cultures . . . So just brainstorming here.	She makes a second attempt to transition to the lesson and succeeds. The students' emotional needs have been met, a positive relationship among students and between teacher and students is in place. The class is entirely with her. In giving the instructions for the Venn diagram exercise, she makes it clear through her choice of words, her self-revision of phrasing, and her inflection (often up), that this is a low stakes exercise where students should freely associate ideas. Thus she is promoting intellectual risk taking.
2:50	*Pause while teacher circulates among students. Several inaudible one-on-one teacher-student conversations.* So I'm just asking you to do this, ah, of what you think you know, which is fine 'cause it's gonna help us with our [work] today. So it's fine that we didn't use this [inaudible] *Pause. Teacher circulating* So just list anything in terms of American culture, and, I hate to say it, but stereotypes that we have of us, stereotypes we might have of Chinese culture, and what we think we have in common. And we'll revisit this throughout our unit to see whether or not we're actually accurate with some of our views or whether, maybe, we're a little bit off.	She clarifies for students that they need not feel certain about the claims they will write down and that, in fact, she anticipates some of them may turn out to be stereotypes. In this way, she continues to foster risk taking. She explains how the results of this exercise are relevant to the lesson, and she explains how all the claims, both the accurate and inaccurate, will be valuable and will be used as part of the learning process later in the unit of study. She thus validates anything and everything that students may write while also acknowledging that at some point, the class will distinguish what is true from what is untrue. Here, she balances the importance of today's intellectual risk taking with the necessity of finding out, ultimately, what's true. (Marie, Humanities 11-12 1302050012)

(T. = teacher; S. = student)

to be revised, about which the teacher said to the class, "I haven't given you a grade. . . . I know that drives you crazy, but I hope it creates incentive . . . this is about learning to write." With small, significant moves like this, the teacher shifted the student focus from compliance with an assignment, to active agency in an authentic task of revision.

The intellectual demands of this class were substantial, the expectation of the teacher was for students to make improvement (revising the essays), which was coupled with the belief that they were capable of doing so and would indeed do so. The class was, also, clearly focused on deeper learning (brainstorming, creating higher level questions).

What is particularly remarkable about the brief observational segment above is that in less than four minutes, the teacher moved the class from a fairly chaotic state of post-vacation boisterousness to a psychologically safe space, a harmonious group, ready and willing to step up to a demanding academic task. As she moved into the academic component, what was remarkable was not so much the techniques she employed, which were entirely appropriate (accessing prior knowledge, explaining the purpose of the lesson, connecting the current task to future tasks, etc.), but the nuanced way she deployed these techniques to achieve more subtle purposes. For example, she used particular phrases ("just preliminary," "similarities that *you think* exist," "just brainstorming here") to lower the stakes of the task, foster free association, and promote intellectual risk-taking. She also regularly inflected her voice up, implying that the exercise is about tentative knowledge not certainty. But she also let students know ("we'll revisit this throughout our unit") that today's answers would not be the final word, that accurate information is the ultimate goal ("to see whether or not we're actually accurate"), and to prepare students for the possibility that their answers today would be wrong ("or whether, maybe, we're a little bit off"), and that possibility is an expected part of the exercise and not a negative mark. All of these moves suggest a teacher with a deep repertoire of teaching strategies, coupled with a powerful social-emotional radar, a strong desire to connect in a relational way with students, and a driving intellectual purpose—a veritable symphony of attributes, likely honed over years of practice, performed with artistry.

Principles of Teaching

The example we just shared is representative of classrooms where an instructional demand for deeper learning was evident across several of our studies. In scrupulously analyzing audio-recordings, transcripts, and field notes, several themes emerged from these classes. We list them below with some explanatory details.

Teachers Focused on Disciplinary Knowledge and Skills Woven Together

Teachers wove skill instruction across all three domains of our taxonomy with development of disciplinary knowledge. In these classes, students were learning fundamental disciplinary knowledge for math, English, social studies, science, and so on; however, they were simultaneously benefiting from instruction in important skills. This was another nail in the coffin for any contention that a focus on skills denies students access to disciplinary knowledge. Likewise, a focus on disciplinary knowledge does not have to crowd out attention to high-level skills. These teachers illustrated clearly that the back-to-basics rallying cry is misguided, and why the skills-vs.-content debate may be put to rest.

It Was the Teacher, Not the Subject

The excellent teaching we observed spanned subjects, grade levels, ability levels, and schools. This suggests that intellectual demand is not the result of the subject taught, the grade level, the academic track, or the school. That leaves the teacher.

Teachers Were Attuned to the Psychological Safety[13] of Their Students, Especially in Diverse Classrooms

Teachers persistently addressed group dynamics and strived to create a harmonious environment, demonstrating an understanding that doing so is a prerequisite to academic learning. Researchers have found that school connectedness is crucial to academic achievement and that relationships matter to student success.[14] What these teachers show us is that the foundation of connectedness is not a program, class, or counselor. Rather, teachers weave it into the everyday fabric of classroom life. Excellent teachers pay attention not only to students' academic qualities but also to their psychological needs in a fluid, continuous process. Particularly in classes of students who are culturally and linguistically diverse, and, often, members of groups marginalized by a white mainstream culture, this attribute is crucial to student success.

Teachers Adapted Their Teaching to the Moment

Teachers consistently matched teaching moves to the dynamic moment in the classroom in ways that fostered harmony and advanced the academic lesson. These teachers showed that having good radar for social-emotional dynamics is not enough. As a teacher, you have to act. These teachers continuously adjusted their teaching in subtle ways as they sensed changes in tone and climate. For example, one teacher responded in a remarkable way to an unanticipated classroom event. The teacher was introducing the lesson to the whole class just after the starting bell, when a student arrived late to class. While continuing to lead instruction, she gestured for the student to sit at an available desk, and, noting that the student appeared chilled, removed her own scarf and wrapped it affectionately around the student's neck as the student took her seat. All while continuing with the lesson.

Teachers Had a Wide Repertoire of Effective Moves

Teachers deployed a variety of moves with stunning fluency and density. It was nearly impossible during the analysis to link a single move to a single purpose. One move dissolved into the next as multiple purposes were served from moment to moment. The expert work of these teachers demonstrates that to teach well—that is, to teach a deep and broad range of skills while also addressing disciplinary knowledge—requires intelligence and practice. It also requires an ability to pay attention to many subtle variables in a complex environment (what we call radar) and an ability to call on a deep repertoire of instructional moves (what we call improvisation).

Instruction Was Tied to Complex Assessments, Often Performative in Nature

Assessments in these classes were often designed by the teacher and included some type of performance or demonstration. They stood in contrast to the more routine test-based assessments or occasional, less demanding "projects" in other classrooms as well as the state-required accountability instruments. As long as on-demand pencil-and-paper tests are the norm in schools, the depth and range of skills taught to students will remain severely limited. The aphorism, "Assessment drives instruction," should be at the forefront of educational planning, from the classroom to the U.S. Department of Education.

Teachers Built Strong Relationships With Students

Teachers exhibited a powerful desire to connect relationally with students, both individually and collectively, and displayed a nearly palpable joy in doing so. The sort of connectedness displayed by these teachers goes well beyond clinical description. There was genuine affection. These relationships benefited teachers as well as students. Because of mutual relationship building, the teachers became more engaged. They clearly felt they had a stake in the successful growth of their students—not just as scholars, but as people.

Notes

1. National Research Council. (2012). *Education for Life and Work: Developing Transferable Knowledge and Skills in the 21st Century*. Committee on Defining Deeper Learning and 21st Century Skills, James W. Pellegrino and Margaret L. Hilton, Editors. Board on Testing and Assessment and Board on Science Education, Division of Behavioral and Social Sciences and Education. Washington, DC: The National Academies Press, 32–34.
2. Performance was determined based on MCAS test scores over time, using a formula that weighted schools by percentage of students eligible for free/reduced meals and non-white.
3. Papers from the five studies are as follows:

   Nehring, J., & Szczesiul, S. (2012). *How Four Educators Navigate the Twin Policy Demands for External Accountability and Twenty-First Century Knowledge: The United States Context*. Unpublished Manuscript.
   Szczesiul, S., Nehring, J., & Carey, T. (2015). Academic task demand in the 21st-century, high-stakes-accountability school: Mapping the journey from poor [to fair to good to great] to excellent? *Leadership and Policy in Schools*, *14*(4), 460–489. doi:10.1080/15700763.2015.1026448
   Nehring, J., & Szczesiul, S. (2015). Redefining high performance in Northern Ireland: Deeper learning and 21st century skills meet high stakes accountability. *Journal of Educational Change*, *16*(3), 327–348. doi:10.1007/s10833-015-9250-8
   Nehring, J., Charner-Laird, M., & Szczesiul, S. (2017). What real high performance looks like. *Phi Delta Kappan*, *98*(7), 38–42. doi:10.1177/0031721717702630
   Nehring, J., Charner-Laird, M., & Szczesiul, S. (2019). Redefining excellence: Teaching in transition, from test performance to 21st century skills. *NASSP Bulletin*, *103*(1), 1–27. doi:10.1177/0192636519830772
   Nehring, J. (under review). *It Matters How You Manage Diversity: Cultural Difference in Northern Ireland's Secondary Schools*.

4. See directly above for full citations of the investigations that made up the UMass Lowell studies.
5. The National Academies of Sciences, Engineering and Medicine. (2011). Defining deeper learning and 21st century skills. *Current Projects*. Division of Behavioral and Social Sciences and Education. www.nationalacademies.org/cp/committeeview
6. National Research Council, *Education for Life and Work*.
7. National Research Council, *Education for Life and Work*, 3.
8. National Research Council, *Education for Life and Work*, 5.
9. Doyle, W. (1983). Academic work. *Review of Educational Research*, *53*(2), 159–199.
10. City, E., Elmore, R., Riarman, S., & Teitel, L. (2009). *Instructional Rounds in Education: A Network Approach to Improving Teaching and Learning*. Cambridge, MA: Harvard Education Press, 30.
11. For discipline specific studies of math, reading, and history, respectively, see the following three papers:

    Cross, D. I. (2009). Alignment, cohesion, and change: Examining mathematics teachers' belief structures and their influence on instructional practices. *Journal of Mathematics Teacher Education*, *12*, 325–346.

Richardson, V., Anders, P., Tidwell, D., & Lloyd, C. (1991). The relationship between teachers' beliefs and practices in reading comprehension instruction. *American Educational Research Journal, 28*(3), 559–586.

VanSledright, B., Maggioni, L., & Reddy, K. (2011, April). *Preparing Teachers to Teach Historical Thinking? The Interplay between Professional Development Programs and School-Systems' Cultures.* Paper presented at the 2011 annual meeting of the American Educational Research Association, New Orleans, LA.

For an excellent review of research on teacher beliefs, overall, see Fives, H., & Gill, M. G. (2014). *International Handbook of Research on Teachers' Beliefs.* Abingdon, UK: Routledge.

12. Thornton, S. J. (1991). Teacher as curricular-instructional gatekeeper in social studies. In J. P. Shaver (Ed.), *Handbook of Research on Social Studies Teaching and Learning* (pp. 237–248). New York: Macmillan Publishers.

13. See:

Kahn, W. A. (1990). Psychological conditions of personal engagement and disengagement at work. *Academy of Management Journal, 33*(4), 692–724. doi:10.2307/25628

Edmondson, A., & Roloff, K. (2009). Overcoming barriers to collaboration: Psychological safety and learning in diverse teams. In E. Salas, G. Goodwin, & C. Burke (Eds.), *Team Effectiveness in Complex Organizations: Cross-Disciplinary Perspectives and Approaches* (pp. 183–203). Abingdon, UK: Routledge.

14. Klem, A. M., & Connell, J. P. (2004). Relationships matter: Linking teacher support to student engagement and achievement. *Journal of School Health, 74*(7), 262–273.

2 Agreement From Policy Leaders

Because our taxonomy was based on a single, comprehensive review of research in psychology and economics, we wanted to see how it squared with other voices in the education sector. We began by reading a number of prominent reports and studies produced in the last three decades that called for deeper learning, called by various names.

Six years after the publication of *A Nation at Risk*, the watershed report of Ronald Reagan's National Commission on Excellence in Education, there was still no clear national direction for K-12 education.[1] A newly elected President, George H.W. Bush, had campaigned on a promise to establish national education goals. To get the ball rolling in a highly visible way, he invited the nation's governors to a summit to be held at Thomas Jefferson's University of Virginia. UVA's classical architecture, stately ash and maple trees, and intellectual ethos, provided the perfect setting to make good on the campaign promise. The Charlottesville summit helped generate political consensus for national educational goals, which the President used to advance his legislative agenda known as Goals 2000.[2]

In tandem with the President's national goals initiative, Secretary of Labor Elizabeth Dole launched a supporting commission in 1990, the purpose of which was to examine labor markets to see how exactly schools would need to prepare students to succeed. The Secretary's Commission on Achieving Necessary Skills (SCANS) produced a report in 1991. *What Work Requires of Schools* identified two conditions that the authors claimed had changed about the world of work, prompting a re-look at what schools should teach, namely, "the globalization of commerce and industry and the explosive growth of technology on the job."[3] The report continued by saying that these changes "have barely been reflected in how we prepare young people for work."[4]

The SCANS report laid out a framework for what schools should teach based on "the findings of cognitive science."[5] It began with the usual list of basics: reading, writing, arithmetic, mathematics, listening, and speaking. But it continued with creative thinking, decision making, problem solving, "seeing things in the mind's eye," "knowing how to learn, reasoning, responsibility, self-esteem, sociability, self-management, integrity/honesty."[6]

Though this list looks much like a dozen other lists of '21st century skills' produced endlessly by various committees, it is important to remember that this was perhaps the first time this range of skills was being invoked as required for all school children in a new economy. Also striking is that the report emphasized that the basics must be taught interwoven with thinking skills and personal qualities. "Students do not need to learn basic skills before they learn problem-solving skills. The two go together. They are not sequential but mutually reinforcing."[7] The integration of basics and thinking skills is a theme that was to dominate subsequent reports from all corners.

Traditionalist critics might, and, indeed, have, criticized the report for its silence on academic subjects. While the point is accurate, it is also important to note that the authors of the SCANS report did not intend to lay out a comprehensive framework for schools. The report focused narrowly and deliberately on the implications of labor market trends for education. The authors were quite clear about this.

> This report concerns only one part of . . . education, the part that involves how schools prepare young people for work. It does not deal with other, equally important, concerns that are also the proper responsibility of our educators. We do not want to be misinterpreted. We are not calling for a narrow work-focused education. Our future demands more.[8]

Though the SCANS report introduced the public to ideas central to what became the '21st century skills' movement, it never actually used the phrase. Its earliest appearance in print, appears to have been a commentary in *Science* magazine by then-candidate for U.S. President, Michael Dukakis.[9] The Commonwealth of Massachusetts, which Dukakis served as governor, is, coincidentally, where our story goes next.

In the early 1990s, three economists became interested in understanding the relationships among schooling, skills, and wages. Richard Murnane and John Willett from Harvard University, and Frank Levy from across the Charles River at the Massachusetts Institute of Technology, began examining two nationally representative databases with information about high school students from the class of 1972 and the class of 1980 (National Center for Education Statistics "National Longitudinal Study of 1972," and "High School and Beyond"). Previous research had demonstrated time and again that educational attainment leads to higher wages, but the three researchers were interested in finding out whether particular *skills*, as opposed to degrees earned, were associated with wage levels. Like the Department of Labor's SCANS commission, their focus was the skills required by the new knowledge economy. By studying data from cohorts approximately a decade apart, Murnane, Willett, and Levy were able to identify correlations between proficiency with basic high school math, the kind taught in most schools by 8th grade, and wages in the first six years after graduation. They found, not surprisingly, there was a wage bump for those individuals proficient with basic math. Digging deeper, however, they found that in more recent years the wage bump for math was spreading to more jobs across the economy. They also found that the portion of the wage bump directly tied to math proficiency was shrinking. These patterns were particularly strong for males. They concluded:

> helping a male graduating from high school in 1980 to improve his math skills would contribute only modestly to increasing his wage level. . . . It is possible that other skills students learn at school or at home have grown in importance in the labor market more than have basic math skills but such skills have not yet been identified.[10]

So what were those "other skills" not yet identified? The researchers were determined to find out. Murnane and Levy, continuing on their own, decided to visit a sample of employers that paid good wages and required this new skill-set, to find out what, exactly, these skills were. What Murnane and Levy discovered was that, increasingly, jobs across many economic sectors, required three things: 1) the "basics"—meaning math, problem solving, and reading—but at a higher level than what most students were attaining by high school graduation; 2) "soft skills"—including "the ability to work in groups with people of different backgrounds and to make effective oral and written presentations," and 3) a facility with computers for simple functions such as word processing.[11] They also found the number of jobs that could be performed without basic math, and without the new "soft" skills, was shrinking. This, they argued, was worrisome from an economic standpoint, meaning a potential for higher unemployment coupled with a shortage of qualified workers. They also worried from the standpoint of a civil society. Democracies flourish when the vast majority can earn a decent living. Civil unrest increases with income inequality. These data were showing approximately half of high school graduates headed for a future in which they would not be able to find sufficient work to make a decent living, let alone raise children. Murnane and Levy's findings were published in 1996 in *Teaching the New Basics*, a book which also featured stories of schools that were beginning to teach the new basic skills. The book was well positioned to influence the national conversation, in part because it was published not by an academic press, but by Free Press, a well-regarded trade publisher, known for books that break new ground in a range of fields. Their work was establishing not only a ground-breaking economic argument, it was making a case for civil society.[12]

Like the National Academies' report and the SCANS report, Murnane and Levy's book argued for an interweaving of basic and complex skills, what they called "the new basics." But their book went further. Murnane and Levy identified promising schools around the United States that were finding inventive ways to rethink traditional school incentives in order to position teachers to teach the new basic skills and to motivate students to learn them. An elementary school in Austin, Texas, joined with community organizers and an interfaith religious group to identify urgent priorities and rally parents, teachers, and students for a schoolwide transformation. A youth apprenticeship program in Boston was launched by a private industry group in cooperation with the public schools. With the potential for a permanent job, students became motivated to excel in school and teachers started teaching the new basic skills required for work placements. Professional learning systems for teachers in Pasadena, California, Southern Maine, and Philadelphia engaged teachers in long-term collaborative teams where they learned how to teach the new basic skills. In all instances, conventional school subjects were transformed with the infusion of higher-level skills, and the transfer of learning to new situations was at the center of the work. It is important to note that many of the examples the authors used were located in urban communities equipping students who might, due to race or class, experience gaps in pay or even opportunity, with the academic and soft skills necessary for success in the shifting economy.

Had talk of a new, important skill set come from professors of pedagogy, it might not have gained traction in the policy mainstream—just more *education reform* talk—but in this instance the United States Department of Labor and several noted labor economists—from Harvard and MIT, no less—were making considerable noise, and the public began to listen.

The appeal of both the SCANS report and Murnane and Levy's book was due, in part, to the fact that they were asking an important, interesting, and straightforward question that people easily connect with: What do you need to know to succeed in the workplace? An equally important question is: What do you need to know to succeed in college? That question became the focus of another study launched several years later by the Association of American Universities.

In 2000, the Association of American Universities and the Pew Charitable Trust jointly sponsored a three-year study to be led by University of Oregon Professor David Conley. The study set out to uncover what high school graduates need to know in order to succeed in college. Over the course of two years, researchers interviewed 400 faculty and administrators from 20 colleges. *Understanding University Success: A Report from Standards for Success* was released in 2003. The report identified skills required "to do well enough in college entry-level core academic courses to meet general education requirements and to continue on to a major in a particular area."[13]

Understanding University Success identified foundational knowledge and standards in six academic areas: English, mathematics, natural sciences, social sciences, second languages, and the arts. Like other reports from this period, Conley's report emphasized the importance of interweaving basic knowledge with complex skills, as well as the importance of transfer. "Understanding and mastery of content knowledge . . . is achieved through the exercise of broader cognitive skills. It is not enough simply to know something; the learner must possess the ability to do something with that knowledge."[14]

In 2002, Conley founded the Educational Policy Improvement Center (EPIC) at the University of Oregon, Eugene, to provide assistance to schools as they transitioned from a content-based curriculum to an approach focused on college and career skills. The combination of the AAU report, the outreach of the EPIC Center, and a number of books and articles authored by Conley in the years following, helped put new ideas about teaching on the minds of educators and policy makers, and it helped put the phrase "college and career ready" on the lips of a reading public.[15] Interest in the cluster of skills later termed "21st century skills" was growing like a snowball rolling downhill. Just one year after Conley's report came out, a very similar report was released by yet another quickly assembled entity.

The American Diploma Project was launched in 2002 as a joint undertaking of three education policy organizations. Achieve, Inc., the Education Trust, and the Thomas B. Fordham Foundation. It was funded in part by the William and Flora Hewlett Foundation, linking it to the bloodline of other studies and reports in this review. The project asked what do higher education leaders and employment recruiters want in the young people they bring to college and the workplace. Researchers interviewed leaders in higher education and employers in fields identified in a preliminary study as growing sectors of the new economy. The report was published in December 2004. *Ready or Not: Creating a High School Diploma that Counts*,[16] began by reciting what was becoming a copy-paste list of concerns over the mismatch between what students are taught and what is needed after graduation. The report then identified "college and workplace readiness benchmarks" in mathematics, English, Workplace Tasks and post-secondary assignments. Strikingly parallel to Conley's "foundations" the ADP's "benchmarks" identified basic knowledge and complex skills across a range of traditional subjects.

Like the other reports, *Ready or Not*, affirmed that school learning needs to be an interweaving of basic subject matter content and complex skills. Unlike other reports, however, this report, advanced a solution rooted in a command-and-control vision of "aligned" standards, required, state-level tests, prescribed course curricula, and "accountability" for results. It was a get-tough prescription for a system viewed as weak and lazy. The Report's recommendation for aligned standards based on "college and career ready" goals, served as the impetus for the development of the Common Core State Standards five years later.

We come now to the final entrant in what at times felt like a growing chorus of school reform ideas all singing in harmony and at other times seemed more like a cacophonous bidding war in competition for the prize of deciding the future of public schooling and getting the credit.

This last entrant was the Partnership for 21st Century Skills, later renamed P21. Organizing members were a mix of education organizations and high-tech companies, including America Online (AOL), the National Education Association, Dell Computers, Apple Computers, Microsoft, and Cisco Systems. In early literature, the United States Department of Education was listed as a "Partner" one level down from the organizing group. Launched in 2002, P21 wasted no time ramping up its profile. It immediately began building a national presence by giving briefings and leading panel discussions for major education groups, such as the National School Boards Association. It also convened forums to advance its agenda, attended by representatives from prominent education entities, such as the Harvard Graduate School of Education, the National Geographic Society, Educational Testing Service, several state departments of education, the National PTA, and relevant trade and professional associations.[17]

With all the hoopla, it seemed to be advancing an agenda before making one, and within a short year, it produced a report, *Learning for the 21st Century*,[18] which presented a framework for knowledge and skills along with a strategy for change. The framework consisted of six imperatives: "emphasize core subjects, emphasize learning skills, use 21st century tools to develop learning skills, teach and learn in a 21st century context, teach and learn 21st century content, use 21st century assessments that measure 21st century skills."[19] The report also recommended next steps for policy makers, parents, businesses, higher education, educational leaders, researchers, and professional organizations. Teachers did not make the list. Like the other reports, *Learning for the 21st Century* advocated for a twin focus on basic subjects and complex competencies, however, unlike several of the other reports, it did not say specifically how this would happen, instead, offering vague practical suggestions for teachers: "examples, applications, and settings from students' lives. . . . bringing in outside experts . . . use the community as a learning laboratory."[20]

P21 was strong on public relations—it was led for many years by public relations expert Ken Kay—and outreach, even though its empirical foundation was mostly derivative. Because of its relentless advocacy, P21, more than any other initiative profiled here, put "21st century skills" on the map for the average American citizen.

So far, our contemporary focus has been on the United States. It turns out the ideas behind "21st century skills" were emerging in other nations with competitive economies.

In 2011, two Dutch researchers, Joke Voogt and Natalie Roblin, set out to review the status of 21st century skills globally.[21] They knew from previous reviews of the literature that the concept did indeed have global currency.[22] What they wanted to find out was the degree to which relevant frameworks aligned and what the status was of implementation and assessment. They examined eight frameworks which they judged most prominent, and 35 studies and reports associated with them. Three of the frameworks were from consortia of several nations and corporations, three were from international organizations (OECD, UNESCO, EU), and three were from the United States.

Voogt and Roblin found that all of the frameworks were in close agreement about what they meant by 21st century skills, very similar to what we saw in the foregoing review of initiatives in the United States. One of the frameworks they studied is P21. But beyond confirming a close alignment, Voogt and Roblin discovered something more interesting related to implementation and assessment: "intentions and practice seemed still far apart" (2012, p. 299). With implementation, they found systems struggle with the massive culture shift required to change what educators and the public believe school to be about. Assessment was facing similar challenges since on-demand tests, which remain the go-to system measure for student learning were not suited to assessment of many 21st century skills.

An international conference on the teaching profession, sponsored by the Organization for Economic Cooperation and Development, and held in Banff, Canada, in 2015, provides further evidence of international interest. The conference report reached conclusions in line with much that we have examined so far, emphasizing the importance of widening teaching repertoires to include a range of pedagogies from inquiry to direct instruction. The report's author, Andreas Schliecher concluded, "What is important are the mixes of pedagogical approaches. Innovation is not about using a single new teaching method or one kind of technology; it is about employing a combination of approaches, including direct teaching, and tools."[23]

All of the reports we reviewed, without exception, acknowledged the importance of students learning both traditional academic subjects and complex skills. All of them also acknowledged that these two things should not be taught separately or sequentially, but woven together. Most of the initiatives pointed out, furthermore, that teaching all these things in a way that empowers students to transfer learning from a school context to new situations, outside of school is essential. All of these features align with the findings of the NRC report, and they were regularly enacted in the teaching of exemplary teachers in our study, constituting a shared vision for teaching—that was largely unacknowledged by anyone. What is also true is that the convergence of ideas in these reports represented a synthesis of ideas from two pedagogical lineages that for generations had been at odds with one another. What these reports advanced and what the excellent teachers in our studies demonstrated is that the rivalry between these two pedagogies was completely unnecessary. Good teaching weaves together elements of both. The rivalry was over. Both sides won.

Notes

1. National Commission on Excellence in Education. (1983). *A Nation at Risk: The Imperative for Educational Reform a Report to the Nation and the Secretary of Education*. Washington, DC: United States Department of Education.
2. For an excellent treatment of education policy and politics during this era see, McGuinn, P. (2006). *No Child Left behind and the Transformation of Federal Education Policy, 1965–2005*. Lawrence, KS: University Press of Kansas.
3. Secretary's Commission on Achieving Necessary Skills. (1991). *What Work Requires of Schools: A SCANS Report for America 2000*. Washington, DC: United States Department of Labor, viii.
4. Secretary's Commission, *What Work Requires*, viii.
5. Secretary's Commission, *What Work Requires*, 16.
6. Secretary's Commission, *What Work Requires*, Appendix C, 32.
7. Secretary's Commission, *What Work Requires*, 16.
8. Secretary's Commission, *What Work Requires*, 1.
9. Dukakis, M. (1988, October 14). Science policy. *Science*, *242*(4876), 173–178. doi:10.1126/science.173-a
10. Murnane, R., Willett, J., & Levy, F. (1995). *The Growing Importance of Cognitive Skills in Wage Determination*. Working Paper No. 5076. Washington, DC: National Bureau of Economic Research, 15. doi:10.3386/w5076
11. Murnane, R., & Levy, F. (1997, February). A civil society demands education for good jobs. *Educational Leadership*, 34–36.
12. Murnane, R., & Levy, F. (1996). *Teaching the New Basic Skills: Principles for Educating Children to Thrive in a Changing Economy*. New York: Free Press.
13. Conley, D. (2003). *Understanding University Success: A Report from Standards for Success*. Eugene, OR: Center for Educational Policy Research. Accessed 2/22/19: https://eric.ed.gov/?id=ED476300, No. ED476300.
14. Conley, *Understanding University Success*, 8–9.
15. Information about the E.P.I.C. Center at the University of Oregon, Eugene, may be found at www.epiconline.org/
16. American Diploma Project. (2004). *Ready or Not: Creating a High School Diploma That Counts*. Washington, DC: Achieve, Inc.
17. Partnership for 21st Century Skills. (2003). *Learning for the 21st Century: A Report and Mile Guide for 21st Century Skills*. Partnership for 21st Century Skills. See Appendix A.

18. Partnership for 21st Century Skills, *Learning for the 21st Century*.
19. Partnership for 21st Century Skills, *Learning for the 21st Century*, 4.
20. Partnership for 21st Century Skills, *Learning for the 21st Century*, 12.
21. Voogt, J., & Roblin, N. (2012). A comparative analysis of international frameworks for 21st century competences: Implications for national curriculum policies. *Journal of Curriculum Studies*, *44*(3), 299–321.
22. See:

> Anandiadou, K., & Claro, M. (2009). *21st Century Skills and Competences for New Millennium Learners in OECD Countries*. OECD Education Working Papers, No. 41. OECD Publishing.
>
> Dede, C. (2010). Comparing frameworks for 21st century skills. In J. Bellanca & R. Brandt (Eds.), *21st Century Skills: Rethinking How Students Learn* (pp. 51–75). Bloomington, IN: Solution Tree Press.

23. Schleicher, A. (2015). *Schools for 21st-Century Learners: Strong Leaders, Confident Teachers, Innovative Approaches, International Summit on the Teaching Profession*. Paris: OECD Publishing, 68.

3 Agreement From Historic and Emerging Pedagogies

For over a century, pedagogical thought has been dominated by two traditions called by various names: on the one hand, traditional, classical, and teacher-centered; on the other, progressive, constructivist, liberal, student-centered. Each represents a loose set of beliefs and teaching practices going back centuries. It makes no sense to call one 'traditional,' as is often the case, as though the other were invented yesterday. We will use the terms 'student-centered' and 'subject-centered' because in one tradition, pedagogy begins with the student and in the other, it begins with academic subjects. In this chapter, we take a brief look at some of the people and ideas forming the lineage for each tradition in order to see how the new, unifying vision for teaching combines elements of both. We also examine the rivalry between the two traditions that has, at times, broken into public debate—a rivalry dissolved by the teachers in our study who regularly drew on both traditions to guide their practice. Finally, we examine the blind spots which have rendered issues of equity and cultural pluralism, until recent decades, nearly invisible to both traditions.

Student-Centered Teaching

The documented tradition of student-centered teaching begins with Jean-Jacques Rousseau. His *Emile*, written as a novel, chronicled the life of a pupil and his tutor. Throughout the book, Rousseau emphasized the importance of curiosity, direct sensory experience, and exploration—Emile's true teachers. The tutor's role was to facilitate the process. Much of the book reads like pages torn from project-based learning. A brief episode illustrates:

> When the child wants to measure the height of a room, his tutor may serve as a measuring rod; if he is estimating the height of a steeple let him measure it by the house; if he wants to know how many leagues of

road there are, let him count the hours spent in walking along it. Above all, do not do this for him; let him do it himself.[1]

The book gained early prominence when both book and author were condemned by the French Parliament, shortly after its publication in 1762, for suggesting all religions were of equal value. A warrant was issued for Rousseau's arrest, and he fled to Switzerland, where *Emile* was again condemned by authorities as a threat to the state and religion. This only elevated the book's prominence. Students in Zurich protested in support of Rousseau.[2] No surprise that, ever since, *Emile* has been a touchstone for liberal educators who emphasize the roles of curiosity and experience and openness to new ideas.

Though government authorities found *Emile* worrisome, the book attracted many contemporary readers, among them a young Swiss named Johann Pestalozzi, who was "seized by this visionary and highly speculative book."[3] Pestalozzi, who struggled initially as a journalist and farmer, went on to found a series of schools through which he developed a distinctive approach to education which, like Rousseau's, featured the child's own curiosity as guiding force and experience as the material for learning. Pestalozzi believed that learning must fully engage the child—"head, heart and hands."[4] He was perhaps the first advocate of teaching "the whole child," a phrase that became popular in the early 20th century.

One of Pestalozzi's students extended and carried Pestalozzi's ideas into the next generation. Friedrich Froebel began his teaching career in Frankfurt, Germany, where he first encountered Pestalozzi's ideas. He later studied under Pestalozzi in Switzerland. He went on to found several schools of his own, and developed his own educational philosophy which he advanced through several books as well as by magazines that he started. Froebel believed that child's play was the essence of learning. He invented kindergarten—the children's garden—as a place within the educational system that featured play. Froebel wrote, "Play is the highest phase of child development . . . play is not trivial, it is highly serious and of deep significance."[5]

A focus on curiosity, exploration, experience, and engagement of the child's full self (intellectual, physical, emotional/spiritual) lay at the core of the educational approach advanced by Rousseau, Pestalozzi, and Froebel. Remarkably, the ideas passed to each person through personal contact. They passed next to German educator, Margarethe Schurz, who encountered Froebel's ideas while studying in Hamburg. She later met Froebel, and assisted her sister in establishing kindergartens in Germany. Later, with her husband, a German political exile, she emigrated to the United States and settled in Wisconsin, where she established the first kindergarten in the United States. It was there that the baton passed once again to an American educator, Elizabeth Peabody. Peabody, a prominent figure in the American transcendentalist movement, had worked as an assistant to Bronson Alcott at his experimental school in Boston—a school that drew on the child's curiosity, while emphasizing reflection and experience. Peabody was taken with Schurz's kindergarten, and subsequently traveled to Germany to study Froebel's ideas. She returned to found more kindergartens in the United States, and advanced the movement with a magazine. The *Kindergarten Messenger* was published from 1873 to 1877. Twenty-first-century skills were advancing nicely, and it was only the 1800s.

At the beginning of the 20th century, the rise of the social sciences, psychology in particular, turned the stream of educational ideas, born in the Romantic era, in a scientific direction. An American, Harold Rugg, was a leading figure in this transformation. Trained as an engineer and psychologist, Rugg brought a sharp quantitative mind to educational studies, during the early decades of the 20th century. A series of studies, led by Rugg during the 1920s, illustrated both his interest in kindergarten and the manner in which he and others were re-casting education in general, in a way that both preserved and modernized the Romantic tradition of Rousseau, Pestalozzi, Froebel, Schurz, and Peabody. In the very first study of the series, Rugg and his colleagues studied the language of 27 kindergarten children, observing each one for 15-minute intervals. Their conclusions, though not exactly stunning, illustrated the scientific thinking that was now being layered over the lineage of educational philosophy started by Rousseau. Rugg wrote that the kindergarten child "is essentially a self-assertive individual; that he is a linguistic experimentalist engaged in using words to become acquainted with the world around him . . ."[6] Rugg's article made early use (maybe the first documented use) of the term "whole child," which, in this article, referred to "the whole study of the whole child in action,"[7] characterizing both the kindergarten curriculum, which attended to many aspects of the child all at once, and the research approach which was equally attentive to many aspects of the child.

Rugg went on to develop a series of textbooks drawing together the subjects of history, geography, political science, and sociology, *Man and his Changing Society*.[8] He invented the idea of a "social studies" curriculum and was a founder of the National Council for the Social Studies, which has continued as a premier national professional association to the present. Rugg's textbooks were notable not only for their integration of several academic disciplines but for their problem-based pedagogy. Rather than presenting valorizing narratives of United States history and society, as was common in textbooks of his day, Rugg's texts presented social problems and invited students to investigate them. At first wildly popular in public schools, Rugg's texts began to fall out of popular favor when critics, led by the American Legion and the Advertising Federation of America, suggested they were unpatriotic and sympathetic toward socialist and communist thought.

The work of scholars like Rugg proceeded hand in hand with a growing movement of school practitioners, which came together in 1919 as the Progressive Education Association. The PEA was an affiliation of like-minded schools around the United States. An early pamphlet laid out principles intended to guide education, including "freedom to develop naturally," "direct and indirect contact with the world and its activities, and use of the experience thus gained," and "correlation between different subjects."[9]

In 1933, the PEA launched a study of progressive schools, the purpose of which was to make the case for progressive education with respect to college admission. 30 schools within the PEA network were tracked for eight years, following students as they moved through the school programs, on to college, and through college. The study found students from progressive schools did as well as their counterparts in conventional schools, and that students from schools with the most progressive practices fared even better.[10]

Unfortunately for progressives, the outbreak of World War II, which coincided nearly to the day, with the release of the findings of the eight-year study, immediately swept away progressive ideals, henceforth seen as experimental and soft, from the public schools, and ushered in an era of educational conservatism, in the name of patriotism and the interest of war preparedness.

Student-centered ideals in pedagogy did not surface again on a national stage until the 1960s, swept back in to favor by a rising tide of reformist social thought, and, indirectly, by the civil rights movement. Experimentation, however, was confined to pockets of liberal thinking. It wasn't until the 1980s and the watershed report of the National Commission on Excellence in Education, "A Nation at Risk," that mainstream attention turned once again to a wholesale re-thinking of schools. Several large-scale studies,[11] undertaken around the same time, focused on secondary education in particular, finding that instruction, in general, across the United States, focused merely on memorization of facts and formulas accompanied by high levels of student disengagement.

Theodore Sizer, author of one of the studies, determined to attempt change in real schools. Founding the Coalition of Essential Schools in 1984, Sizer laid out nine "common principles" reminiscent of long-standing student-centered ideals, but cast in language that appealed to a mainstream public. The Coalition's Principles sounded like common sense:

> [T]he school should focus on helping young people learn to use their minds well . . . curricular decisions should be guided by the aim of

thorough student mastery and achievement . . . teaching and learning should be personalized to the maximum feasible extent. . . . The diploma should be awarded upon a successful final demonstration of mastery.[12]

The Coalition grew over three decades to include 1,100 schools across the United States and beyond.

But times change. The great tectonic plates of federal education policy were shifting in the 1990s. Liberal support for education funding had run up against a Republican agenda to control domestic spending. At the very start of the new 21st century, a grand compromise was reached in which Republicans agreed to more education spending at the federal level as long as states and localities were held accountable for results. Thus, with the No Child Left Behind Act of 2002, new federal money flowed to schools, but annual testing became a mandate for all children across the country. With the new testing focus, schools began to hunker down and teach "the basics," meaning, content-heavy, recall-and-application-level tasks, as the means to boost test scores. For movements like the Coalition of Essential Schools, this meant a slow death. The deeper learning which CES schools advanced, particularly in high need communities where the Coalition was having perhaps its greatest impact,[13] was wholly unrecognized by a system that recognized only lower-level cognitive skills. The Coalition persevered, but faced with dwindling foundation support in an era of test-based accountability, it was forced to close its national office in 2016.

Though testing and accountability were the dominant forces in policy and practice through the first decade of the new century, a separate, countermovement was coalescing, driven by a growing recognition that the emerging knowledge economy needed workers who were good at more than following instructions and performing simple, routine tasks—an unintended outcome of the accountability movement. Work from scholars like Murnane and Levy, and awareness-raising reports from the American Diploma Project and the National Research Council, began to shift attention once again.

Separately, interest in interpersonal and intrapersonal skills was gathering around the idea of "social-emotional learning." The Collaborative for Academic, Social, and Emotional Learning (CASEL, www.casel.org) served as a research and advocacy organization. Though it began in 1994, its influence grew as educators and the public became frustrated with the relentless focus on testing. Likewise, the Association for Supervision and Curriculum Development, in conjunction with the United States Centers for Disease Control and Prevention, launched its "whole child" initiative in 2007, the purpose of which was to "change the conversation about education from a focus on narrowly defined academic achievement to one that promotes the long term development and success of children."[14]

Terms like 'progressive,' 'whole-child,' and 'student-centered' are slippery because individuals and movements appropriate them for their own purposes, place them within differing narratives. and give them differing definitions. The recent cluster of terms, including new 'basic skills,' '21st century skills,' 'college and career readiness,' and 'deeper learning,' are experiencing a similar lexicographic journey. A more detailed review would explore these nuances.[15] That said, the broad patterns outlined here, hold over time. We should also point out that presenting a short outline, as has been done here, risks creating the impression that there was a single stream of thought cascading down through the ages—which is not the case. While the personal links among some of the educators profiled is remarkable, it is important to note there were many other educators doing similar work who are not mentioned here. Nothing has been said, for example, about Maria Montessori, the Reggio Emilia approach, G. Stanley Hall, to name just a few of the figures that could have been included. We've also made no mention of John Dewey, who towered over educationists of the 20th century. Our purpose here is to sketch an outline.

The teachers in our study drew on the student-centered tradition when they focused on relationship-building, student engagement, the psychological dynamics of the class, and assessments that are performative. The themes in the reports we have reviewed implicate the student-centered tradition in their attention to interpersonal skills such as collaboration and teamwork, and intrapersonal skills such as flexibility and metacognition. But that is not to say these skills are absent from the subject-centered tradition, which we review next. Though each tradition emphasized certain elements, their fullest expressions invoke all of the skills advanced with the deeper learning construct in different ways—which is why the new, unifying vision for teaching is able to draw on both and dissolve the rivalry between them.

Subject-Centered Teaching

People say it's 'academic' when a question is interesting but irrelevant. They say 'trivial' when it fundamentally doesn't matter. Both terms are associated with the tradition we explore next. 'Academics' are the academic subjects, the scholarly disciplines, historically associated with schooling—such as math, history, and science. 'Trivial' refers to the trivium, which was the first series of courses that students took in medieval universities. The derision points to a criticism that the subject-centered tradition has frequently heard, namely, that its approach to education is remote from matters of the real world. Advocates of a student-centered pedagogy have seized on this point, overzealously, to make their case for teaching that starts with the direct experiences of the student.

Subject-centered teaching has roots in higher education as opposed to the student-centered tradition, the roots of which lie in child rearing and the education of young children. This makes sense when you consider the philosophical stance of each—start with the academic disciplines vs. start with the child.

Subject-centered teaching was first consolidated in the medieval European universities as a seven-course sequence divided into two parts. There was the trivium, consisting of grammar, rhetoric, and logic, to be followed by the quadrivium, made up of music, arithmetic, geometry and astronomy. Universities in the middle ages sprang from cathedral schools which had been established during the earlier middle ages by the church to train clergy. With time, the children of nobility began to attend cathedral schools, numbers grew, the curriculum became more advanced, and the full seven-course sequence became the norm in universities across major European cities. During the Renaissance, humanist thinkers modified the curriculum, adding history, Greek, and philosophy. The curriculum was also called 'liberal arts' and 'classical.'

The subject-centered tradition began to move beyond the cathedral schools and university settings in the 1700s. A major figure in this transformation was Frederick the Great, King of Prussia, who as an act of state-building established a public education system by decree, in 1763, with compulsory attendance for both boys and girls, to be supported by taxation. But it wasn't until a generation later that the so-called Prussian system, influenced heavily by Wilhelm Von Humboldt in the Prussian ministry of the Interior, began to fold in elements of the academic tradition. Humboldt, a classicist by training and his own scholarship, brought a strong humanistic and even Romantic element to the classical tradition. Anthony Grafton, a Humboldt scholar at Princeton, wrote that for Humboldt, "learning was not a mass of facts but a properly formed mind."[16] It's not especially surprising to learn that in his role as Director of Ecclesiastical and Educational Studies in the Prussian Department of the Interior, Humboldt sent teachers to Switzerland to study Pestalozzi's methods.[17] In an essay, penned early in his career, Humboldt wrote, "In learning, everything is connected."[18]

Humboldt, along with many scholarly contemporaries, sought to create an intellectually powerful and technically competent German state by establishing a meritocratic system of education. Teachers were to be properly trained and supervised, and uniform tests were to be administered to all students (the 'abitur'). However, rote learning was by no means the goal. Humboldt believed in the power of language and history to enlighten the mind. He sought a kind of revisionist classicism that revered history and ancient languages while honoring each child's personal genius. Prussia's king, Frederick William, thought otherwise. More interested in centralized control than classical learning, he kept Humboldt's administrative innova-tions (exams, supervision of teachers, etc.) and curricular organization, but rejected the spirit of academic freedom that inspired them. Under Frederick William, the seeds of the modern public school were planted: social effi-ciency, centralized control, nationalistic focus, quality assurance through formal training, supervision, exams, and an ethos of conformity. The idea of a classical/academic education was added only as a veneer.

It was to Germany and especially Berlin, the capital of Prussia, that many American educators travelled during the 19th century to learn from the national system. The Prussian influence on the formation of public school-ing in the United States was pivotal. But Berlin did not represent a mono-lithic view of schooling. Scholars and schools located there represented a range of educational philosophy from the free-spirited kindergartens of Froebel to the nationalistic system instituted by Frederick William. Ameri-can visitors took from Germany what they wished. Elizabeth Peabody took kindergarten and transplanted it to the United States. Francis Parker, a New England school man, took the Romantic ideals of Froebel and Pestalozzi and created a pedagogy that he introduced in Quincy, Massachusetts, where he served as superintendent and gained a national following. William T. Harris, first United States Commissioner of Education, studied in Germany, and Horace Mann, the first Secretary of Education for the Commonwealth of Massachusetts, visited there in 1843.

Horace Mann is, in both symbol and substance, the most significant 19th-century American reformer when it comes to the establishment of organizational features that shaped American public schooling. Appointed as Secretary for the newly established Massachusetts Board of Education in 1837, most of the organizational features that Mann advocated were adopted statewide by mid-century. Crucial to the consolidation of Mann's agenda was a six-month trip he took to Europe. In 1843, the Board of Edu-cation granted him leave to travel, at his own expense. He visited schools in Belgium, Holland, France, England, Scotland, Ireland, and Germany. Judg-ing from his widely publicized *Report*, Mann was clearly most impressed with Germany and Prussia in particular. He stated:

> Arrange the most highly civilized and conspicuous nations of Europe in their due order of precedence, as regards the education of their peo-ple, and the kingdoms of Prussia and Saxony, together with several western and south-western states of the German confederation, would stand preeminent, both in regard to the quantity and the quality of instruction.[19]

What Mann admired in Prussia and, to a lesser extent, elsewhere was the idea of a "national system," Prussia happened to have, in his view, the best. Elements he admired are named in his *Report*: "universal attendance," "compulsory attendance," "supervision of the schools" (p. 88), "a uniform system of instruction" (p. 89), "the establishment of a board of education who should exercise a supervisory power over the books to be used" (p. 89). His admiration extended to the organization of classes in schools. "Children are divided according to ages and attainments; and the single teacher has charge only of a single class, or of as small a number of classes as is practical" (p. 115). Mann's report on his European trip was serialized in the twice monthly *Common School Journal*, published in Boston (and founded by Mann for dissemination of his views), taking up the entirety of eight issues including an "extra" and filling a total of 131 pages. Due in no small part to Mann's relentless advocacy, all of these features, except for a truly national system, eventually found their way into schooling in Massachusetts and, eventually, across the United States.

Academic subjects, the heart of the subject-centered tradition, were also part of the Prussian system. In his report, Mann went on at length about teaching methods in each subject, which included: reading, arithmetic and mathematics, grammar and composition, writing and drawing, geography, Bible history and bible knowledge, music, "exercises in thinking," "knowledge of nature," "knowledge of the world," "knowledge of society." Most or some of the last four, Mann said, were present in every school.

Mann made clear his belief in the value of a competent, well-trained teacher in his damning remarks on the monitorial system (older students teach younger students so fewer teachers are needed) which he observed in England, Scotland, and Ireland: "One must see the difference between the hampering, blinding, misleading instruction given by an inexperienced child, and the developing, transforming, and almost creative power of an accomplished teacher" (p. 99). Mann mentioned France, Belgium, Ireland, and Holland as other places besides Germany where there was a national system of education. The only country, he wrote, where he did not observe a national system was England. "And it is the country where, incomparably beyond any other, the greatest and most appalling social contrasts exist" (p. 86).

In both the European national systems that Mann observed and the emerging American system there was a blending of a subject-centered educational tradition with the state-building goal of social efficiency. The subjects Mann enumerated bear the marks of the trivium and quadrivium. The insistence on compulsory attendance and the regime of close supervision and uniform exams were the means of an efficiency-seeking state. Though largely decentralized, an American system of education, rooted in that model, emerged in the latter part of the 19th century and early decades of the 20th century. It has remained largely intact: age-graded, subject-based, time-regimented, exam-driven. Education historian David

Tyack has observed that so ingrained have these features become, they are a kind of "grammar" of schooling, the inviolable rules for what constitutes a real school.[20]

The coupling of state efficiency and the subject-centered curriculum continues to draw advocates in our own times. In 1984, E.D. Hirsch, an English professor at the University of Virginia, published *Cultural Literacy: What Every American Needs to Know*.[21] Hirsch argued, much like Mann a century and a half earlier, for a common, subject-based curriculum as the bulwark of a strong republic. The book was widely read, and Hirsch established the Core Knowledge Foundation and a network of Core Knowledge schools that remains active.

When the teachers in our study teach the concepts and methods of the academic disciplines, they draw on the subject-centered tradition. When the studies and reports we review emphasize the importance of domain-based knowledge and weaving-together of basics and higher-level skills, they are invoking elements that are central to the subject-centered tradition.

The student-centered tradition of learning that pulses through the centuries with advocates and reformers from Pestalozzi to Sizer, emphasizes thinking skills required to explore and make sense of the student's own experience. The subject-centered tradition, rooted in the medieval university and popular today with initiatives such as the Core Knowledge Foundation, emphasizes domain-based knowledge that provides a frame for interpreting experience. Each tradition provides something essential. What's 'new' about the new, unifying vision apparent in the practice of exemplary teachers in our study and the themes emphasized in the reports we reviewed, is the recognition that a truly excellent education draws on fundamental elements of *both* traditions.

A Complete Pedagogy

Schooling is not enacted in a cultural vacuum. The two pedagogical traditions under review developed in the context of societies that were profoundly racist and classist. Both traditions were dominated by educators from privileged backgrounds, focused largely on privileged groups. While there is wisdom in the principles and practices each tradition forged, they represent an incomplete pedagogy. To the extent that non-dominant groups were included, cultural assimilation was almost always the assumed goal, based on a deficit view of non-dominant cultures. Cultural annihilation was not beyond the scope of mainstream educators, as in the case of the state education of Native Americans.[22] The emphasis on uniformity, advocated by Horace Mann and others, foreclosed any attention to cultural pluralism. Though scholars of color, such as Booker T. Washington and

W.E.B. Dubois, occasionally broke into the white-dominated canon of education, participation in the framing of curriculum and organizational systems largely excluded anyone outside the dominant culture.

In the United States, this began to change with the Civil Rights movement in the 1950s, which led to more robust and public critiques of the form and function of education and this country.[23] Early leaders made their presence known in practice, academia and policy. Freedom schools, organized to confront resistance to Brown v. Board of Education, sprang up in Boston, New York City, Virginia, and Mississippi. The freedom schools were highly participatory and focused on voter registration, civic engagement, academic subjects, social change, and black history. In academia, John Ogbu lanced the myth of meritocracy with an analysis of race as caste.[24] James Banks conducted early work on the experience of black students in the classroom and black history.[25] The 1970s saw increased attention to cultural pluralism with a rising generation of scholars of color and white allies committed to the investigation of cultural and linguistic diversity in schools and related social justice issues. The result was a blossoming of scholarship and pedagogy aimed at affirming the cultural identities of students while promoting academic success. Deliberately dismissing the historic goal of assimilation, the new perspective took the label, "multicultural education."[26] Subsequent scholarship by Gloria Ladson-Billings, Django Paris, and others introduced pedagogies committed to affirming and nurturing the home cultures and emerging identities of students.[27] Norma Gonzalez and her co-authors countered an historic deficit view of students from non-mainstream cultures with their notion of "funds of knowledge."[28] Based on action research by teachers who ventured into the homes and communities of their students, they argued that, because people everywhere are essentially competent, they construct knowledge from their environment and children come to school with it. The work of educators is to gain an understanding of the "funds of knowledge" with which their students are already equipped, and build on them.

By the 1990s, there were signs that the scholarship of pluralism and social justice was influencing white leaders within the mainstream pedagogies. For example, in 1996, the Coalition of Essential Schools added a 10th Common Principle focused on equity and diversity.[29] Also, E.D. Hirsch, who had been sharply criticized for advancing a Eurocentric canon with "cultural literacy," emphasized in later works the empowerment of black students and other marginalized groups through access to literacy in the dominant culture. Though his perspective remained controversial, it represented an evolution from his earlier thinking.[30] We note also that the 2015 International Summit on the Teaching Profession, discussed earlier, though dominated by Westerners, included organizations with global reach such as the Organization for Economic Cooperation and Development and Education International with representation in 170 countries and territories.

The most capable teachers in our study showed a commitment to cultural pluralism, an interest in the lives of their students, and a respect for the experience their students brought to the classroom. They folded those dispositions into a practice that drew as well from the subject-centered and student-centered traditions to create the basis of a complete pedagogy representing a powerful, new, unifying vision for teaching and learning.

Throughout the last two centuries, as educational leaders worked to centralize systems and create common curricula, we must recognize the effects on students of color of attending schools that taught a curriculum predominantly designed by and representative of a white experience in the country and the world. This lack of representation had and continues to have stark effects on students of color, and other students from non-dominant backgrounds, to this day.

Notes

1. Rousseau, J. (1921). *Emile, or Education* (M. A. Barbara Foxley, Trans.). London and Toronto: J.M. Dent & Sons; New York: E.P. Dutton. Accessed 10/12/17: http://oll.libertyfund.org/titles/2256#Rousseau_1499_500, paragraph 500.
2. Pestalozzi, J. (1894). *How Gertrude Teaches Her Children* (L. E. Holland & F. C. Turner, Trans., E. Cooke, Ed., Intro. and Notes). Syracuse, NY: C.W. Bardeen, xvi. Accessed 2/22/19: https://archive.org/stream/howgertrudeteach00pestuoft/howgertrudeteach00pestuoft_djvu.txt
3. Pestalozzi, *How Gertrude Teaches Her Children*, xvi.
4. Johann Heinrich Pestalozzi. www.jhpestalozzi.org/
5. Frobel, F. (1908). *The Education of Man* (W. N. Hailmann, Trans.). New York: D. Appleton and Company, 54–55. Accessed 2/22/19: https://archive.org/stream/educationofman00fruoft#page/n3/mode/2up
6. Rugg, H., Krueger, L., & Sondergaard, L. (1929). Studies in child personality: I. A study of the language of kindergarten children. *Journal of Educational Psychology, 20*(1), 1–18. Excerpt from the abstract.
7. Rugg, et al., Studies in Child Personality, 1.
8. Rugg, H. (1937). *Man and His Changing Society*. Boston: Ginn and Company.
9. From Progressive Education Association. (1924, March). The principles of progressive education. *Progressive Education Magazine.* www.parkschool.net/files/park100fppforweb02-28-2013.pdf. For a fuller treatment of the origins of progressive education, see Reese, W. (2001). The origins of progressive education. *History of Education Quarterly, 41*(1), 1–24. Reese points out there was a popular, gushy, saccharine side to the movement, which John Dewey took pains to point out as well. Reese concludes that progressive education succeeded "in wreaking havoc on the schools."
10. Aikin, W. (1942). *The Story of the Eight-Year Study*. New York: Harper.

11. Boyer, E. (1983). *High School: A Report on Secondary Education in America.* New York: Harper & Row.
Goodlad, J. (1984). *A Place Called School.* New York: McGraw-Hill and Sizer, T. (1984). *Horace's Compromise: The Dilemma of the American High School.* Boston: Houghton-Mifflin.
12. Coalition of Essential Schools, Ten Common Principles. See www.essential schools.org for the full list of Common Principles and information about the Coalition of Essential Schools founded by Sizer.
13. See Meier, D. (1995). *The Power of Their Ideas: Lessons for America from a Small School in Harlem.* Boston: Beacon Press.
14. The Whole Child. www.wholechildeducation.org.
15. For a full treatment of progressive education in the context of American K-12 schooling in the late 19th and 20th centuries, see the following two works:

> Cremin, L. (1964). *The Transformation of the School: American Progressivism, 1876–1957.* New York: Vintage.
> Kliebard, H. (1986). *The Struggle for the American Curriculum, 1893–1958.* New York: Routledge.

16. Grafton, A. (1981). Wilhelm von Humboldt. *The American Scholar, 50*(3), 371–381.
17. Entry: Wilhelm von Humboldt, Baron. (1998). *Encyclopedia of World Biography*, Gale. *Biography in Context*, Accessed 11/10/17: libraries.state.ma.us
18. From an essay written in 1792, cited in Grafton, Wilhelm von Humboldt.
19. Mann, H. (1843). Mr. Mann's seventh annual report: Education in Europe. *The Common School Journal, 6*, 5–12, 84.
20. Tyack, D., & Tobin, W. (1994). The grammar of schooling: Why has it been so hard to change? *History of Education Quarterly, 31*(3), 453–479.
21. Hirsch, E. D. (1987). *Cultural Literacy: What Every American Needs to Know.* Boston: Houghton Mifflin.
22. Smith, A. (2003, November). Soul wound: The legacy of Native American schools. *Amnesty Now,* 14–17.
23. Though the civil rights movement advanced the idea of school desegregation, scholarship has shown that the threat of desegregation was used widely in the south by whites to eliminate the jobs of black educators. See Fultz, M. (2004). The displacement of black educators post-Brown: An overview and analysis. *History of Education Quarterly, 44*(1), 1–27.
24. Ogbu J. U. (1978). *Minority Education and Caste: The American System in Cross-Cultural Perspective.* San Diego, CA: Academic Press.
25. Banks, J. A. (1971). Teaching Black history with a focus on decision making. *Social Education, 35*(7), 740–745, 820–821.
26. Banks, J. A., & McGee, C. (2015). *Multicultural Education: Issues and Perspectives* (9th ed.). Hoboken, NJ: Wiley.
27. Ladson-Billings, G. (2014). Culturally relevant pedagogy 2.0: a.k.a. the remix. *Harvard Educational Review, 84*(1), 74. Also, Paris, D. (2012). Culturally sustaining pedagogy: A needed change in stance, terminology, and practice. *Educational Researcher, 41*(3), 93–97.
28. Gonzalez, N., Moll, L., & Amanti, C. (2005). *Funds of Knowledge: Theorizing Practices in Households and Classrooms.* Mahwah, NJ: Lawrence Erlbaum Associates.
29. "The school should demonstrate non-discriminatory and inclusive policies, practices, and pedagogies. It should model democratic practices that involve

all who are directly affected by the school. The school should honor diversity and build on the strength of its communities, deliberately and explicitly challenging all forms of inequity." Accessed 2/22/19: http://essentialschools.org/common-principles/

30. Hirsch, E. D. (2010). *The Making of Americans: Democracy and Our Schools.* New Haven: Yale University Press.

4   Agreement From Contemporary Research

As our awareness of the consensus about good teaching grew, we recognized that while policy reports and historic traditions are important sources of knowledge, we needed also to look at the best contemporary research on pedagogy. If we were to sample some large-scale studies, would we find agreement with the sources we'd already interrogated, or would we find something completely different?

We began with the work of John Hattie. For many years, Hattie has carried on a kind of Holy Grail quest to define teaching excellence. Frustrated, like many, by the steady stream of quick fixes, the tidal churn of school reform movements, and the pendulum swing of education policy, Hattie aspired to gather all the empirical evidence he could find to answer enduring questions about the nature of effective teaching practice. Problem was, how do you dig through thousands upon thousands of studies carried out in widely varied contexts using widely varied methods to uncover common principles?

For assistance, he turned to a relatively new statistical method for comparing obscenely large numbers of studies, a method introduced in the 1970s by Gene Glass, a statistician at the University of Colorado. When it was introduced, the "meta-analysis" represented a revolutionary turn in the traditional idea of the literature review. In a dramatic keynote speech before the American Educational Research Association in April of 1976, Glass described a new approach to making sense of a large number of studies focused on a given topic—the meta-analysis. Meta-analysis accomplished this by calculating a numerical effect size for a given intervention on an outcome, and then comparing effect size across any number of studies, particularly a very large numbers of studies. The mathematical details of meta-analysis go beyond our purposes here, but we will note that since its introduction in 1976, it has stood up to global scrutiny and become a staple of social science research.

Hattie seized on meta-analysis as the vehicle of choice for his massive quest, as did many other researchers in education. This meant that Hattie was not limited by his ability to assemble studies to create his own meta-analyses; he could, in addition, pull together meta-analyses conducted by others. Meta-meta-analysis. In 2010, based on 15 years of research, Hattie published *Visible Learning*, which presented findings from over 50,000 research studies analyzed in 800 meta-analyses.[1] The book identified effect size for 138 influences on learning across six domains (student, home, school, teacher, curricula, and teaching approaches). Reviews rightly called the book "ground-breaking" and "definitive." It truly was both.

A Meta-Meta Analysis

Early in the book, Hattie offers some broad conclusions. Prominent among them is the recognition that teaching excellence is a deliberate and artful blend of subject-centered and student-centered approaches. We agree, and we quote below the relevant passage in full because of its significance to our work and because of its clarity. Italics have been added to underscore the relevance to our argument in this book.

> The model of visible teaching and learning *combines, rather than contrasts*, teacher-centered and student-centered learning and knowing. Too often these methods are expressed as direct teaching versus constructivist teaching (and then direct teaching is portrayed as bad while constructivist teaching is considered to be good). Constructivism too often is seen in terms of student-centered inquiry learning, problem-based learning, and task-based learning, and common jargon words include "authentic", "discovery" and "intrinsically motivated learning." The role of the constructivist teacher is claimed to be more of facilitation to provide opportunities for individual students to acquire knowledge and construct meaning through their own activities and through discussion, reflection and the sharing of ideas with other learners with minimal corrective intervention. . . . These kinds of statements are almost directly opposite to the successful recipe for teaching and learning (Hattie, p. 26).

Among Hattie's findings, we see strong confirmation of the themes uncovered in our own much more modest studies. In what follows, we pair themes uncovered in the UMass Lowell studies with Hattie's findings from his meta-meta-analysis.

Teachers Were Attuned to the Psychological Dynamics of Their Students, and Teachers Built Strong Relationships With Students

We place these two characteristics together because the first is a prerequisite for the second. Hattie's analysis found a large effect size for specific teacher attributes here including empathy, warmth, and encouragement (p. 119).

Teachers Had a Wide Repertoire of Effective Moves, and Teachers Adapted Their Teaching to the Moment

Again, we place two characteristics together because the first is a prerequisite for the second. And, again, we see close correlates in Hattie's findings. "Adept at improvisation," and "problem solving disposition to teaching," both had strong effect sizes (p. 117).

Instruction Was Tied to Complex Assessments, Often Performative in Nature

Hattie does not report on formal assessment per se. On the one hand, this would appear to make sense. Assessment reveals outcomes and is the measure of achievement, which is the premise of Hattie's argument. It would therefore not be a variable in any of the studies he draws on. On the other hand, we know that the nature of assessment has a powerful influence on the nature of instruction. It therefore makes perfect sense to examine different forms of assessment and how they impact learning. Doing so, however, using Hattie's approach would lead only to a tautology.

Nonetheless, Hattie reports on two related variables. One is "providing formative evaluation," and the other is "frequent/effects of testing." Formative evaluation, it turns out, has an enormous effect size according to Hattie's analysis. Among the 138 variables identified, it ranks third with an effect size of 0.90. Formative evaluation is the kind of feedback a coach gives on an ongoing basis, and coaching is what performative assessment requires. As for testing, Hattie concludes that when tests are used strategically to inform instruction (as a feedback mechanism), they can boost student learning, but when administered for other reasons (such as accountability), they can result in unintended consequences such as a narrowing of the curriculum.

We see close linkages between the findings of the UMass Lowell studies and selected findings from Hattie's enormously scaled analysis. What about Hattie's many other findings, that is, characteristics of teaching not addressed in the UMass Lowell studies? There are, frankly, quite a lot, too numerous to elaborate here and also already quite well known. For example, "teacher clarity," "classroom management," "goals," and "time on task," are all significant levers for learning. We refrain from examining these elements here for several reasons. First, many are already well known from the teaching effectiveness literature. Second, many are associated with studies in which large scale, standardized exams are the tool that measures learning. One of the fundamental premises of the UMass Lowell study and this book overall is that such research shows us how to teach for test success yet leaves us completely in the dark about what it takes to teach for deeper learning. When we seek corroboration between the UMass Lowell studies and the Hattie study, we do so with this skepticism in mind, since Hattie does not report how dependent his findings are on test-based achievement studies. Third, the UMass Lowell studies were designed to identify teacher characteristics in classrooms where instructional demand was observable across the three domains (cognitive, interpersonal, intrapersonal). Many of the teaching strategies Hattie identifies are quite simply what instructional demand looks like within these domains. For example, "meta-cognitive strategies," "study skills," and "self verbalization/self questioning" are teacher moves that, when authentically deployed would count, in the UMass Lowell studies, as instructional demand in the intrapersonal domain. Knowledge of these specific moves is potentially very useful to teachers, and we encourage readers to read Hattie themselves.

Hattie's work is perhaps the most comprehensive study of teacher practice ever undertaken. His findings helped to corroborate our growing conviction that there is strong agreement across many players in the education sector as to what constitutes exemplary teaching. Yet, we wondered, were there studies that, like ours, looked specifically at teaching for deeper learning? If so, what did *they* find? Our studies were relatively small. Was there, perhaps, a study with a large sample that looked at the same elements of deeper learning? There was.

At the same time that the National Academies was trying to make sense of the 21st century skills initiatives, the William and Flora Hewlett Foundation in Menlo Park, California, launched a related project. Hewlett's newly hired education director, Barbara Chow, was keen to develop a concept that she called "deeper learning." In an *Education Week* essay published in October 2010, Chow described deeper learning with five key attributes:

1) Mastery of core academic content.
2) Critical thinking and problem-solving.
3) Working collaboratively in groups.

4) Communicating clearly and effectively.
5) Learning how to learn.[2]

Backed by the considerable resources of the Hewlett Foundation, Chow set out a grant making agenda designed to increase the presence of deeper learning skills and knowledge in classroom instruction. As part of this effort, Hewlett partnered with the American Institutes for Research (AIR) for proof-of-concept research. Over the course of three years, AIR produced three studies of deeper learning. To identify schools that were designing instruction to foster deeper learning, Hewlett looked to a number of school networks committed to outcomes consistent with the deeper learning construct as developed by Hewlett. They identified ten that met their criteria. The first study that came out of the Hewlett-AIR partnership, described the criteria for selection:

> They needed to have experience in, and an explicit focus on, promoting a deep understanding of content and the kinds of competencies reflected in the Hewlett Foundation's identified dimensions of deeper learning, and they needed to do this across whole schools serving diverse populations of students (rather than targeting only certain portions of the students or teachers in a school).[3]

The Hewlett-AIR studies, it appeared, would be, for our purposes, the perfect complement to Hattie's work. Hattie shows us the contributions of individual elements of excellent teaching. Hewlett-AIR shows us how all those factors come together in real schools. As with Hattie's work, we found in these studies, strong alignment with the findings of the UMass Lowell study, major themes in the policy reports we've reviewed and elements of the several pedagogies we've examined. What Hattie and Hewlett-AIR show us is that, in addition to *agreement* that the deeper learning construct constitutes good teaching, there is powerful evidence from large-scale, formal research for the *efficacy* of deeper learning.

Many of the networks in the Hewlett-AIR studies had roots in progressive school traditions (student-centered), and were driven by practitioners who had founded or led innovative schools. For example, one of the ten networks, Big Picture Learning, was founded by Dennis Littky, a charismatic school principal passionately focused on student-centered learning who, early in his career, led schools in New York and New Hampshire. He became active in the Coalition of Essential Schools during the 1980s and 1990s, where he worked closely with Deborah Meier, Theodore Sizer, Howard Fuller and other progressive school leaders. In 1995, Littky and colleague Elliot Washor founded the Metropolitan

Regional Career and Technical Center in Providence, Rhode Island, which quickly became a haven of hope for young people marginalized by mainstream schools.

The pedagogical foundation of "The Met" was the "advisory," a micro-community of 15 students and a teacher-mentor. Multiple advisories made up the school. The mentor helped each student design an educational plan around the student's interests and a workplace internship. The Met quickly gained a reputation for turning around lives. Ideas and practices pioneered at the Met School spread. Funders, including the Bill and Melinda Gates Foundation, supported the work, and Big Picture Learning was born.

The Big Picture website lists 51 schools in its network (www.bigpicture. org). Other networks in the Hewlett group came from a techy background, founded by innovators and educators with a digital technology focus. Though close cousins intellectually to progressives like Littky, their pedagogical roots were in the digital revolution and the perceived new teaching and learning demands of a globalized, high-tech world. High Tech High is an example of this kind of network. In 1998, a group of business leaders in the San Diego area met to discuss education in the region. They decided they wanted to create an innovative high school. Taking the lead was Gary Jacobs, former director of education programs at Qualcomm. He teamed with Larry Rosenstock, a former teacher and school leader with a vocational orientation, who had become a national leader in innovative school design. With Gates funding, High Tech High was opened as a public charter school in San Diego in 2000. Like The Met, High Tech High focused on internships, advisories, personalization, and collaboration, but with a strong tech focus. Its successful approach led to replication and the establishment of a network of 13 schools.[4] The ten networks that became the focus of the Hewlett-AIR studies are below.

Asia Society—http://asiasociety.org/international-studies-schools-network
Big Picture Learning—www.bigpicture.org/
ConnectEd—www.connectedcalifornia.org/
EdVisions Schools—www.edvisions.com/
Envision Schools—www.envisionschools.org/
Expeditionary Learning—http://elschools.org/
High Tech High—www.hightechhigh.org/
Internationals Network for Public Schools—http://internationalsnps.org/
New Tech Network—www.newtechnetwork.org/
New Visions for Public Schools—www.newvisions.org/ [5]

In some ways, the Hewlett-AIR studies were like the UMass Lowell studies. Rather than deducing exemplary teacher practice from high test scores, AIR found places that were teaching the full range of skills and examined what they were doing and how they did it. To be sure, AIR was also interested in outcomes since it was contracted to carry out a proof-of-concept study, but the first study in the series they produced focused extensively on teacher practice in schools across the ten networks. What did practice look like in these schools? To what extent did it match up with what we found in the exemplary classrooms we observed? That is the question we turn to next.

What is immediately striking about instruction in the Hewlett-AIR schools is the nearly universal reliance on project-based learning (18 of 19 schools) and widespread use of workplace internships (14 of 19 schools) as anchors for instruction. Projects were often interdisciplinary and rooted in contemporary issues. They often spanned weeks or months and developed knowledge and skills from multiple disciplines. Here's a prominent example.

> Juniors at one school . . . engaged in an in-depth study of a West Virginia coal mining disaster—a case study that tied into a year-long focus on the impact their generation could have on the world. They explored the implications of this one incident and related policies and resources before launching into a study of the United States' dependence on fossil fuels. Students picked a particular issue related to energy use and completed a public policy research paper and presentation, which often involved collecting original data and analyzing them to support their arguments. They also wrote a white paper and made presentations to local experts (such as university professors, politicians, or nonprofits in the sector). This portion of the project integrated both group work and an opportunity to pursue an individual passion. To complement the focus on energy, students also studied West Virginia history, the Great Depression, and related literature and music (e.g., bluegrass). Finally, the project included a trip to coal country in West Virginia, where students immersed themselves in local culture, interviewed local residents, and completed a Habitat for Humanity project. Following the trip, students created multimedia oral histories of the people they interviewed and then showed the compilation at a local gallery, as well as in West Virginia.[6]

Disciplinary learning from this project included science, history, political science, and arts & humanities. Students had an introduction to relevant disciplinary skills, such as conducting a literature review, writing a policy brief, examining historical documents, interviewing, exercising aesthetic judgment, and organizing a multimedia presentation. Collaboration was also evident and, though unstated, long range planning and time management would clearly be required to master all the elements of a project this extended and complex. In summary, the full range of deeper learning skills were getting a serious workout.

Internships at these schools were also a regular feature of the student experience. They were often designed to match the learning goals for an individual student. They involved careful planning in advance of the internship and, afterward, structured reflection and assessment.

> [O]ne network school had several internship programs related to bioscience careers facilitated by two internship coordinators. All students in Grades 11 and 12 at this school were required to conduct internships and were expected to incorporate their internship work into their senior exhibition (a graduation requirement). One internship program at this school was a selective three-year program (from Grade 10 through Grade 12) at a local children's hospital that eased students into working in this environment. They also offered internships with other local hospitals, as well as an internship with a local radio/ television station that focused on how to construct public health announcements and report a health-related story.[7]

What is especially of note is that the internships were not an elective course. Typically, *all* students in the schools in this study were required to participate, thus exposing all students, not just those in a higher track, to the deeper learning demands associated with a well-structured internship experience.

Reading example after example of projects led us to wonder, to what extent, if any, do these strongly student-centered schools include disciplinary learning? While *methods* associated with disciplines are typically required for student projects (for example, interpreting primary sources in history, analyzing empirical data in science), did students experience sufficient *guidance* in developing the methods? Cognitive psychologists are quick to point out that the methods associated with a discipline are different altogether from the teaching required to foster learning of those methods. Epistemology is not pedagogy.[8] To learn the epistemology associated with a discipline and to become fluent with the specific methods that issue from a disciplinary way of knowing requires training, not merely an opportunity to hazard a try. Hattie's work supports this squarely, and scholarship going back to the 1980s has focused on this issue.[9] Lee Schulman invented the term, "pedagogical content knowledge," to signal it.[10] It may well be that students in the Hewlett-AIR study experienced sufficient guidance based on pedagogical content knowledge, but the study does not clearly tell us the extent. Alternatively, it may be the case that these largely project-oriented schools would do well to incorporate more domain-based learning.

Evidence suggests that the vast majority of schools in the Hewlett-AIR study were rooted in the student-centered tradition. At the same time, they folded in elements of the subject-centered tradition that allowed them to meet the criteria for deeper learning, which demands disciplinary learning, higher level skills, working with others, personal capabilities, and transfer. It also merits noting that many of the schools in the networks included in the study serve high need urban populations. That students from historically marginalized groups are gaining access to deeper learning is a huge win for equity and cultural pluralism.

To the larger question of pedagogy, The Hewlett-AIR study raises an important question: If some student-centered schools can meet the deeper learning standard by folding in elements of disciplinary learning, can some subject-centered schools meet the deeper learning standard by folding in elements of the student-centered tradition? That's the question we turned to next, and the answer is yes.

Subject-Centered Schools, Too

In 1924, a new school was established in Geneva, Switzerland, with "eight students and a rabbit."[11] Founded by educators with an international focus, the International School of Geneva was philosophically aligned with *éducation nouvelle*, the European expression of progressive educational principles that enjoyed a heyday in both the United States and Europe in the 1920s. The school flourished for decades and became a model for international education, serving the children of diplomats and expats. In 1968, teachers at the school organized an examination board for international schools, and the International Baccalaureate (IB) was born. IB became a certifying agency for schools that sought IB credentialing. There are now close to 5,000 IB schools worldwide.[12] IB schools follow a prescribed curriculum and graduation is based on standardized exams across a range of academic subjects. Given the program's student-centered progressive roots and subject-focused academic curriculum, it is an interesting hybrid of educational philosophy. Does it have a deeper learning focus? Is it an example of a kind of school that is organizationally academic, but with enough elements of student-centered pedagogy to foster deeper learning?

The IB Diploma Program (DP) consists of course sequences in six subjects and the "DP core." It is in the learning objectives of the subjects and the "Core," especially, that we find a deeper learning focus. The Core consists of three elements. The first is a course called "Theory of Knowledge" described by IB as "a thoughtful and purposeful inquiry into different ways of knowing, and into different kinds of knowledge."[13] The course aims to "make students aware of the interpretative nature of knowledge, including personal ideological biases—whether these biases are retained, revised or rejected." It is assessed with an oral presentation and an essay. The second element of the Core is the Extended Essay, an "independent, self-directed piece of research, finishing with a 4,000-word paper." The student works with a teacher who serves as tutor. The third component is "Creativity, Activity, and Service." Intended as ongoing activity throughout the program, the CAS focuses on the arts, creative thinking, physical exertion, healthy lifestyle, and voluntary service with a learning benefit. Students are expected to regularly reflect on their CAS experiences and complete a CAS project which is not formally assessed. The IB Core clearly focuses on key elements of deeper learning, providing substantial practice with high level cognitive skills, collaboration, and intrapersonal skills. The Theory of Knowledge course shows particular attention to epistemologies of academic disciplines.

In addition to the Core, IB students take courses in six subject areas. Course activities and objectives suggest substantial opportunity for students to practice the full range of deeper learning competencies within a discipline specific context. The biology course for example provides "opportunities to design investigations, collect data, develop manipulative skills, analyse results, collaborate with peers and evaluate and communicate their findings," while exploring content knowledge that ranges from the cell to ecosystems.

A number of recent research studies attest to the achievement benefits and deeper learning opportunities associated with the IB.[14] As a lever for equity, reviews of IB are mixed. Unlike schools in the Hewlett-AIR studies, IB schools are selective, required by the IB organization to have an admission policy, and schools may offer single courses to students outside of the diploma program. IB programs in U.S. high schools are often one of several curricular options, i.e., not the required program for all students. While African-American students graduating from IB programs have been shown to find greater success in post-secondary education, IB has been criticized for establishing an elite brand reinforcing social division.[15]

As with any network or school model, there are no doubt good and bad exemplars of IB schools. What's clear, however is that the IB system, which is strongly discipline-based, makes the point that deeper learning can be achieved in a subject-centered school that thoughtfully folds in elements of the student-centered tradition.

Hattie's work and the Hewlett-AIR studies, along with the NRC review, provide empirical support for the deeper learning construct. They show that the *agreement*, from numerous policy reports, about what constitutes good teaching stands on a solid foundation of research. Our brief look at the

International Baccalaureate also demonstrates that deeper learning can grow within both subject-centered and student-centered schools. With this confirmation of the efficacy of deeper learning, we wondered next why deeper learning is not more widely enacted in schools. We had some hunches, but we wanted to go to a variety of sources to test them empirically. We began by looking at patterns over time, long spans of time. What has teaching looked like not just over the last ten or 20 years, but the last hundred, and what are the forces that have constrained teachers from teaching a deeper skill set than the thin diet of recall and application?

Notes

1. Hattie, J. (2009). *Visible Learning: A Synthesis of over 800 Meta-Analyses Relating to Achievement*. New York: Routledge.
2. Chow, B. (2010). The quest for deeper learning. *Education Week*, *30*(26), 22–24. Though the term 'deeper learning' appears in published sources in the field of education going back to the 1960s, Chow's prominent use of the term in this article and in the subsequent grant program she led appears to have established the contemporary meaning of the term as the set of skills and dispositions viewed as important to school-based learning but often absent from classroom practice. Personal correspondence with Chow suggests that the National Research Council work cited in Chapter 1, endnote 1 also played a role in establishing the term as it is now widely used.
3. Huberman, M., Bitter, C., Anthony, J., & O'Day, J. (2014). The shape of deeper learning: Strategies, structures and cultures in deeper learning network high schools. *American Institutes for Research*. www.air.org and *The Research Alliance for New York City Schools*. www.steinhardt.nyu.edu/research_alliance. Accessed 8/19/17: www.air.org.
4. *Voice of San Diego*. (2006, September 2). Questions for Larry Rosenstock. Accessed 1/11/18: www.voiceofsandiego.org/topics/news/questions-for-larry-rosenstock/
5. Huberman, et al., *The Shape of Deeper Learning*, 5.
6. Huberman, et al., *The Shape of Deeper Learning*, 13–14.
7. Huberman, et al., *The Shape of Deeper Learning*, 16.
8. Kirschner, P., Sweller, J., & Clark, R. (2006). Why minimal guidance during instruction does not work: An analysis of the failure of constructivist, discovery, problem-based, experiential, and inquiry-based teaching. *Educational Psychologist*, *41*(2), 75–86.
9. Bransford, J., Brown, A., & Cocking, R. (Eds.). (1999). *How People Learn: Brain, Mind, Experience, and School*. Washington, DC: National Academies Press.
10. Shulman, L. (1987). Knowledge and teaching: Foundations of the new reform. *Harvard Educational Review*, *57*(1), 1–22.
11. International School of Geneva. Website: www.ecolint.ch/overview/our-history
12. International Baccalaureate. Website: www.ibo.org/programmes/find-an-ib-school/
13. All quotes in this paragraph and the next are from the International Baccalaureate website.

14. See, for example:

> Saavedra, A. (2016). Academic civic mindedness and model citizenship in the International Baccalaureate Diploma Programme. *The Social Studies, 107*(1), 1–13.
>
> Saavedra, A. (2014). The academic impact of enrollment in International Baccalaureate Diploma Programs: A case study of Chicago Public Schools. *Teachers College Record, 116*(4), 6.
>
> Frank-Gemmill, G. (2013). The IB Diploma and UK university degree qualifications. *Journal of Research in International Education, 12*(1), 49–65.

15. See, for example:

> Gordon, M., Vanderkamp, E., & Halic, O. (2015). International Baccalaureate programmes in title I schools in the United States: Accessibility, participation and university enrollment. *IB Research.* www.ibo.org/globalassets/publications/ib-research
>
> Bunnell, T. (2010). The International Baccalaureate and a framework for class consciousness: The potential outcomes of a "class-for-itself".' *Discourse: Studies in the Cultural Politics of Education, 31*(3), 351–362.

Part II

Why Don't All Teachers Teach This Way?

5   How Most Teachers Teach and Why

In 1981, an associate professor at Stanford University took on a question that had nagged him for years. A former teacher, principal, and superintendent, he wondered why most classrooms he had observed throughout his career were 'teacher-centered' and whether it had always been that way. To him, teacher-centered meant a classroom dominated by teacher talk, with students' desks in columns and rows, responding to mainly factual questions, and content rooted in a textbook. Such teaching would tend to demand mostly recall level thinking, very little higher-level thinking, and virtually no demand for interpersonal skills or intrapersonal skills.

Previous studies had speculated about the nature of teaching 50 and a 100 years ago based on old textbooks and curriculum materials, but no one had attempted to establish empirically what went on in classrooms, mainly because there were no easily accessible records. He would have to be enterprising. He ended up reviewing a widely eclectic range of archival sources from the 1890s to 1980, piecing together evidence involving 6,000 teachers. The resulting paper was published in 1983 in the journal, *Theory into Practice*, under the title, "How Did Teachers Teach, 1890 to 1980." The answer that author Larry Cuban found, in what has become a landmark study, and later a book,[1] was that—despite waves of school reform and policy pendulum-swings and education fads over nearly 100 years—the vast majority of public- school classrooms in the United States at both the elementary and secondary levels were persistently teacher-centered. This was a genuinely significant finding because, until Cuban's study, historical work on schools tended to draw on curriculum and policy materials, newspapers, journals, and magazines to learn about schools. But because Cuban had long-term experience working in schools, he knew that printed curriculum materials, textbooks, and reports do not necessarily reflect what happens daily in classrooms. That's why Cuban bypassed the usual approach and went right to evidence of actual classroom practice wherever he could find it—ultimately achieving an impressive database of observed behavior for the 6,000 teachers he tracked down.

What Teachers Taught 20 Years Ago

What about the years since 1980? Is it possible that reform efforts, to which classroom practice had been largely impervious from 1890 to 1980, have, in more recent decades, produced some changes? To answer this question we turned to several studies produced during the last 40 years that are broad enough in scope to give us a sense of the United States as a whole, and sufficiently demanding in their methods to produce credible claims.

In the late 1990s, Robin Henke, a researcher at MPR Research Associates, led a team in a study intended to uncover the broad patterns of how teachers across the United States at the elementary and secondary levels were teaching day to day.[2] The study was sponsored by the National Center for Education Statistics and was based on the results of NCES's national Teacher Follow-up Survey administered by the NCES during the 1994–1995 school year. The survey, administered to approximately 4,000 elementary and secondary teachers across the United States, included questions about teaching practices, instructional materials, homework, and assessment. The survey spanned all subject areas and included teachers from kindergarten through 12th grade. Henke's analysis painted a complex picture of teaching practice 15 years after the end of the period featured in Larry Cuban's study. Key findings included the following: Most teachers across all grade levels reported using teacher presentations, small group work, and whole class discussions on at least a weekly basis. Across all grade levels, textbooks were more prevalent than use of supplementary/original source materials. Approximately 60% of teachers reported that they had students work on problems that had more than one answer or method of solution in a given week. Overall, 57% of teachers reported using portfolios of student work as an assessment instrument in the previous semester. These figures reveal a blend of subject-centered and student-centered practices across content areas and grade levels—even as subject-centered practices persisted as instructional staples. Looking deeper into the results, however it is also clear that student-centered practices were more frequent among the elementary grades. Frequency of small group instruction was higher among teachers of lower grades as was use of supplementary materials beyond a textbook. Additionally, elementary teachers were more likely to use portfolios of student work for assessment purposes. Most striking of all, elementary school teachers were more likely to engage students in higher order thinking tasks than secondary teachers. Overall, Henke's analysis of the NCES survey results suggested that the needle was starting to move with respect to instructional reform. While the 90-year period covered by Cuban's study showed doggedly persistent subject-centered practices despite wave after wave of curriculum reform, the picture of schooling in 1995 suggested change, beginning mainly at the elementary level—perhaps the beginning of a trend.

The possibility of a trend, however was called sharply into question by another study that was completed about the same time as Henke's. In the 1990s, James Stigler, professor of psychology at the University of California Los Angeles, began a collaboration with the National Center for Education Statistics to video record classrooms. During the 1994–1995 school year, the same year as the survey that Henke analyzed, the NCES carried out a project in which 231 8th-grade math lessons in three countries— United States, Japan, and Germany—were videotaped. The project was designed to capture nationally representative lessons and included 81 videotapes of American classrooms. Stigler led the analysis. The findings were devastating. By comparison to Germany and Japan, the U.S. math lessons were largely incoherent, jammed with too much content, and operated at a much lower level of cognitive demand. American teachers required students to engage in procedural thinking at most. Most American lessons began with the teacher demonstrating a problem, followed by students attempting examples, with the goal of students mastering the procedures without attention to conceptual understanding. In contrast, the typical Japanese lesson began with students being presented with a problem, then the teacher provided an opportunity for students to invent solutions, followed by the whole class collaborating to discuss and validate various acceptable approaches—in short, a lesson that called on a range of cognitive skills and interpersonal skills.

What was particularly damning about the Stigler study is that room for alternative interpretations was dramatically reduced by the nature of the data. For the first time, we had a large sample of American classrooms on video. These were not archival photographs or observational notes, as with Cuban's study, or self-reports from a survey, as in Henke's study. Researchers could watch the class in action.

If Henke's findings were cause for hope that schools were beginning to respond to calls for change, Stigler's findings raised enormous doubt as to whether any change was really taking hold. Together, the Henke and Stigler studies suggested continuity with Cuban's findings, namely, that classroom practice which remained mostly subject-centered, with some notable exceptions, from 1890 to 1980 was continuing in roughly the same vein well into the 1990s. What about the decades since?

What Teachers Teach Now

The year 2002 was pivotal for elementary and secondary education in the United States due to passage of the No Child Left Behind Act. The new law represented a grand compromise between Congressional Democrats and Republicans. Democrats wanted more federal funding for schools as an anti-poverty measure. Republicans wanted less federal involvement in schools because it infringed on states' rights and because, in the conservative view, any attempt at social provision by government was inherently inefficient and therefore frowned upon. A compromise was reached when Democrats agreed to "accountability" for public schools that reluctant Republicans insisted upon if they were going to sign over more cash. They, the Republicans, wanted to see results, a return on investment. The measure of success would be student scores on tests to be administered to every child every year they attended school. The Act, passed in late 2001, reflected these fundamentals. All states were required to administer annual exams to all children attending public schools in mathematics and reading or language arts. After a roll-out period of several years, tests would have to be administered annually in each of grades 3–8 and once during years 10–12. If student participation in the exams fell below 95%, states and localities would risk losing federal education funding. Furthermore, the law stipulated that tests must be "statistically valid and reliable." In addition, all state accountability systems were required to "include sanctions and rewards, such as bonuses and recognition, [which] the State will use to hold local educational agencies and public elementary schools and secondary schools accountable."[3] The impact of NCLB was immediate and transformative. States hastily put end-of-year tests in place that, often crudely, met the "valid and reliable" criteria. Test items tended to focus on factoids and simple procedural skills. Schools and teachers, fearing sanctions, focused instruction on test-prep and narrowed the curriculum to emphasize tested subjects while expanding the instructional focus on facts and formulas (e.g. math formulas, formulaic essay writing). Meanwhile non-tested subjects were pushed to the margin of the school day and thinking skills received less attention in daily lessons. In 2007, five years into NCLB implementation, the Center on Education Policy, a Washington based, non-partisan policy institute, surveyed 349 school districts across the nation to gauge the impact of NCLB on curriculum and instruction. CEP researcher Jennifer McMurrer, who authored the resulting paper, found a 43% increase in time devoted to math and ELA since 2001, the year before enactment of NCLB and a corresponding 32% decrease in non-tested subjects, including social studies, science, art and music, physical education, lunch and/or recess. The study also found 84% of districts had substantially altered curriculum to emphasize content in tested subjects.[4]

Because the new battery of tests coming from state education departments emphasized factual content, it is reasonable to infer that thinking skills were, by and large, not part of the curricular overhaul in most districts. Other studies during the first decade of NCLB confirm that hunch.[5] Our own foray into schools demonstrates that many teachers navigated the

conflicting demands for test performance and 21st century skills with pedagogy that invoked the *language* of deeper learning while merely adding
content ("more stuff") or procedural complexity ("more steps").

Just when it looked as though American classrooms might be shifting
their instructional focus toward thinking skills in the 1990s, along came
NCLB, which almost immediately pushed schools and classrooms back
to the teacher-centered approach described by Larry Cuban as dominant
since the 1890s. What emerges, therefore, over the period of 120 years of
instruction in American classrooms is a flat trend line of content heavy,
teacher-centered instruction.

A brief, important side-note here: Cuban's notion of "teacher-centered"
is *not* synonymous with our term, "subject-centered." Cuban's term aligns
roughly with our observation in the majority of classrooms in our series
of studies where only three skills were developed: recall, application, and,
sometimes, analysis. As we've seen, "subject-centered" teaching, as we
have used it, can invoke the full range of deeper learning skills.

Our short history of teacher practice makes it clear that the teachers in our
study are in the minority both across the profession today and across time.
What it does not make clear, exactly is why. Though it alludes to political forces and professional norms, it cries out for a fuller analysis. Many
observers of education have puzzled over this problem. Looking at both
the history and the array of explanations, we see five related theories that,
together, provide a credible, multi-causal analysis.

Theory I: The Manufacturing Metaphor

Since the dawn of the Industrial Revolution in the early 1800s, the means
and ends of industrial manufacturing have influenced to greater or lesser
degree the means and ends of schooling. Over 100 years ago, industrial
manufacturing established a framework for the organization of economic
production so compelling that we quickly began to apply it to other aspects
of culture, failing to acknowledge its logical limits and the potentially harm-
ful consequences of its misuses. The history of public schooling in the United
States may be understood as the tragic misapplication of industrial thinking to human growth and learning. That we continue to conceive of schools
in terms of industry even in a *post*-industrial society speaks to the enduring power of the manufacturing metaphor to make satisfying (if ultimately
disastrous) sense of the world. The problem is that widgets don't think and
people do. Widgets are inert. Children live and breathe—a truth as simple
as it is overlooked. The day that school committeemen (and they were men)
of the 19th century began to draw comparisons between the red brick buildings in town that produced boots and guns and the red brick buildings that

"produced" children was the day that an educational Rubicon was crossed. And as children, increasingly, during the closing decades of the 19th century and the early decades of the 20th century, were organized like parts in a factory, age graded, processed through standardized curricula, shuttled from room to room for fastening on this set of facts and the other set of facts, and as their teachers became laborers responsible for an ever-narrower set of tasks, all parties to the work—pupils and their teachers—were expected to think less and fall in line more. It didn't matter that all the fastened-on facts, like parts, fell off as soon as the product was out the showroom door. What mattered was the process itself, which *looked like* the great and worthy production method of the factory. It made sense there; surely it made good sense here too. Because of the power of economic life, the factory became a dominant metaphor for social relations generally and, therefore, defined much in the life of schools.[6]

Theory II: The Grammar of Schooling

In the early 1990s, historians David Tyack and William Tobin directly confronted the question: Why has the organization of schooling remained so durable over decades despite numerous reform attempts? They found their answer in the power of the received culture. Any reform, in order to succeed broadly across the entire culture, would have to move the public to reconceive the collective conception of a "real school." Tyack and Tobin demonstrated through a series of case studies that efforts to do away with such widely accepted features as Carnegie units and age grading failed not because they were illogical, but because they violated the public's deeply rooted image of what a school is. These deep roots are what Tyack and Tobin called the "grammar of schooling." They concluded that while changing the grammar is exceedingly difficult, it is not impossible through sustained political action and broad social movements. Tyack and Tobin demonstrated that once the manufacturing metaphor had become embedded in the culture, it was there to stay.[7]

Theory III: Social Reproduction

In the 1970s, several academics independently and simultaneously published theoretical works suggesting that schools, by and large, prepared students for future jobs based on their social class. If that were true, then the very idea of schools as an engine for opportunity within a meritocracy would be exposed as a lie. Sam Bowles and Herbert Gintis, economists at the University of Massachusetts Amherst reviewed statistics on educational attainment, IQ, and labor markets to demonstrate that family background had far more to do with the social class a person occupied in adulthood than IQ or academic achievement. Their findings were published in book form in 1976 under the title, *Schooling in Capitalist America: Educational Reform and the Contradictions of Economic Life.*[8]

A year later, the translation of a work by French sociologist Pierre Bourdieu, first published in French in 1970, made its debut in the English language. Bourdieu argued that a person's place in society was determined by a complex web of social relations determined largely by, and reinforcing the continuation of, their social class of origin. Furthermore, schools played a significant role in this process of cultural reproduction—a reproduction of social inequality.[9]

A third work was published the same year presenting a similar stance. Michael Apple, on the faculty of education at the University of Wisconsin, published a study of kindergartners in which his chief finding was that the learning process of the early months of kindergarten were fundamentally a socialization into the norms of work in an industrial society. Tracing the genesis of American public-school organization to theories of social control, Apple made a powerful case for the economic logic behind a curriculum that was first and foremost about listening, following rules, and getting work done.[10]

All three of these works received considerable attention, and they stimulated a junior faculty member at Rutgers University to go a step further in finding broader empirical support for this new critical perspective. Jean Anyon identified five public elementary schools in New Jersey located in communities representing different social strata. During a single school year, she clocked a total of 150 hours observing several 5th-grade classrooms in each school. Clear patterns emerged. In the "working class" school, work was a punishing tedium without explanation as to its purpose. In the "middle class" school, work was about getting the right answer and following instructions. In the "affluent professional" school, work involved creative activity, individual thought and expressiveness. In the "executive elite" school, work focused on developing analytical power and "producing intellectual products that are both logically sound and of top academic quality"[11] Anyon's findings could not have been clearer. Schools in her sample were reproducing social class patterns by defining students' relationship to work and power and capital in ways that matched the social class of their parents. The four categories Anyon identified represent, in descending order, attention to the range and depth of skills in the NRC taxonomy and the practice of exemplary teachers in our study. Students in the executive school were exposed to the full range, while students in the working-class school received a diet of academic task demand similar to what the majority of students in our study experienced. Anyon's paper, despite its small sample size, went on to have enormous scholarly impact.

Together, the critical theory scholars (Bowles & Gintis, Bourdieu, Apple, and Anyon), extended the Tyack and Tobin view. Tyack and Tobin argued that there is a deeply embedded concept of "real school" that reproduces itself from generation to generation. The critical scholars, Anyon especially, revealed that the concept of "real school" depends on one's social class.

Theory IV: White Supremacy

The analysis offered by Bowles and Gintis, Bourdieu, Apple and Anyon explains patterns based on social class in capitalist societies generally, but to understand teaching patterns in the United States requires that the analysis be extended to race and ethnicity. Critical race theory (CRT) inverts conventional civil rights assumptions that racial discrimination is the exception to be addressed by law by asserting that racial animus in the United State is, in fact, the norm for white people and correcting it is a far more complex task than legal recourse can ever achieve. CRT has evolved from work in the area of legal studies pioneered by Derrick Bell and Richard Delgado[12] to include a wide range of academic disciplines and social institutions. It has been applied to public schooling by writers such as Edward Taylor, David Gillborn, and Gloria Ladson-Billings.[13] CRT scholars point to persistent social injustices as evidence: the mass incarceration of people of color, police shootings of unarmed black males, hate crimes against people of color, the concentration of students of color in under-resourced schools, the over-representation of students of color in school disciplinary referrals, special education, and lower track classes, the re-emergence of school segregation, persistent achievement gaps, and the daily micro-aggressions experienced by people of color in a white-dominated society. Extending the work of Anyon and the other scholars in our Theory III, above, CRT explains why white students, who tend to be in better-resourced schools and sit in higher track classes, are exposed to a fuller range of skills in the NRC taxonomy than students of color who attend under-resourced schools, occupy lower tracks, and attend special education classes.

Theory V: High Stakes Testing

The accountability movement, dating back to the 1980s, culminated with the passage of the No Child Left Behind Act in 2002. With the law, high stakes testing quickly became the norm in public schools across the United States. As we have seen, the result was to solidify existing patterns of low-level instructional demand while perhaps widening the learning gaps between privileged and marginalized groups with respect to deeper learning skills, which have gone largely unmeasured and unnoticed by the system.

While the case has been made by others for one or another of these five theories, we argue that each offers a partial explanation for a complex phenomenon which is best understood from multiple angles. The factory created a cultural trope that extended beyond economic institutions. The "grammar" thus established had sticking power across generations and became self-perpetuating. Furthermore, the "grammar" is different depending on the social class of the surrounding community. And the norms of white supremacy actively oppress people of color in society generally and in schools specifically. Finally, high stakes testing has, more recently, solidified the pattern of low-level instructional demand. We believe that efforts to bring about change need to take into account the full and complex web of forces that support the dominant system. Perhaps the most urgent force holding back the full expression of deeper learning across *all* public schools, and all students in them, is the absence of a commitment to cultural pluralism, that is, the failure to see and act upon the truth that diversity makes us stronger.

The history is clear: for generations the classroom norm in the United States has been low-level intellectual demand with little deliberate focus on non-cognitive skills. Teachers who teach a broader and deeper skill-set are in the minority. Access to deeper learning is particularly limited for students of color and other non-dominant groups. The reasons for the persistence of these patterns is complex, rooted in socio-economic forces beyond the schoolhouse and long- standing routines within. Patterns hundreds of years in the making cannot be reversed swiftly and easily, and efforts by educators to impact the broader society are limited by the cultural reach of schools. That said, schools are a good place to begin mainly because of their *potential* for cultural reach. The question is *how* to begin? In the remainder of this book, we argue for working three powerful levers: cultural pluralism, student assessment, and organizational development.

Notes

1. Cuban, L. (1983). What did teachers teach? 1890–1980. *Theory into Practice*, *22*(3), 159–165. Also, Cuban, L. (1993). *How Teachers Taught, Constancy and Change in American Classrooms*. New York: Teachers College Press.
2. Henke, R., Chen, X., & Goldman, G. (1999). *What Happens in Classrooms? Instructional Practices in Elementary and Secondary Schools, 1994–95 (NCES 1999–348)*. Washington, DC: U.S. Department of Education.
3. United States Department of Education. (2001). *Reauthorization of the Elementary and Secondary Education Act: No Child Left Behind*. Title I, Part A, Section 1111, Subsections A and B. Accessed 1/9/18: www2.ed.gov/policy/elsec/leg/esea02/pg2.html#sec1111
4. McMurrer, J. (2007). *Choices, Changes, and Challenges: Curriculum and Instruction in the NCLB Era*. Washington, DC: Center on Education Policy.

5. See, for example,

>Moon, T., Brighton, C., Jarvis, J., & Hall, C. (2007). *State Standardized Testing Programs: Their Effects on Teachers and Students*. University of Connecticut and National Research Center on the Gifted and Talented.
>Hinde, E. R. (2003). The tyranny of the test: Elementary teachers' conceptualizations of the effects of state standards and mandated tests on their practice. *Current Issues in Education, 6*(10).
>Lucey, T., Shifflet, R., & Weilbacher, G. (2014). Patterns of early childhood, elementary, and middle-level social studies teaching: An interpretation of Illinois social studies teachers' practices and beliefs. *The Social Studies, 2014*(105), 283–290.

6. This paragraph is adapted from Nehring, J. (2009). *The Practice of School Reform: Lessons from Two Centuries*. Albany, NY: SUNY Press. See, especially, pp. 2–3 and Chapter One: The Manufacturing Metaphor.
7. Tyack, D., & Tobin, W. (1994). The "grammar" of schooling: Why has it been so hard to change? *American Educational Research Journal, 31*(3), 453–479.
8. Bowles, S., & Gintis, H. (1976). *Schooling in Capitalist America: Education and the Contradictions of Economic Life*. New York: Basic Books.
9. Bourdieu, P., & Passeron, J. (1977). *Reproduction in Education, Society, and Culture*. Thousand Oaks, CA: Sage Publications.
10. Apple, M. (1977). What do schools teach? *Curriculum Inquiry, 6*, 341–358.
11. Anyon, J. (1980). Social class and the hidden curriculum of work. *Journal of Education, 162*(1), 67–92, 83.
12. Delgado, R., & Stefancic, J. (2001). *Critical Race Theory: An Introduction*. New York: New York University Press.
13. Taylor, E., Gillborn, D., & Ladson-Billings, G. (2009). *Foundations of Critical Race Theory in Education*. New York: Routledge.

Part III
System Support

6   Pluralism

Cultural pluralism has been viewed by the dominant culture for generations as an impediment, for which the solution was assimilation, exclusion, and annihilation. What scholars of multiculturalism have been teaching us all in recent decades is that pluralism is a resource; inequity is diminished, and education and democracy thrive, when we learn with and from each other across diverse cultures.

One of our studies focused specifically on cultural diversity, asking how a school might manage the diversity of students it serves in ways that positively impact students' identity formation, academic learning, and their embrace of cultural pluralism as a resource for a richer life and a richer democracy. To answer these questions, we turned to an unlikely place.

Northern Ireland is made up of the six northern-most counties on the island of Ireland. Like the rest of Ireland, these counties are largely a beautiful patchwork of green meadows bounded with stone walls, and coastal cities that make a living from the sea. But Northern Ireland's six counties are not part of the nation called Ireland. Instead, because of a complicated and troubled history, they are part of the United Kingdom. We turned to Northern Ireland as a site for our research partly because, in some important respects, education there is a more intense version of patterns observable in the United States. Northern Ireland serves as a kind of mirror that shows us an altered version of ourselves—with important differences. High stakes testing, a fairly recent system level feature of U.S. schools, has a long history in Northern Ireland. Also, the difference in academic achievement between privileged and marginalized groups in Northern Irish schools is even greater than the United States. Sectarian strife in Northern Ireland—the historic tension between Catholics and Protestants—has achieved levels of violence that in recent decades has rivaled the violence of America's racial tension.

Studies of schooling in Northern Ireland have examined the benefits and challenges of school-based integration of students from backgrounds that are culturally diverse *and* woven together in a legacy of conflict. Integration in Northern Ireland is achieved by three means. Some schools are formally integrated, meaning that they participate in a government scheme that requires roughly equal enrollment of students from Catholic and Protestant families. Integrated schools enroll approximately 6% of all students. Another approach, called Shared Education, assists segregated schools in cooperating across the cultural divide by offering selected classes and professional development jointly, while remaining substantially separate. A third approach, is the unintentional and circumstantial enrollment of students from Catholic and Protestant backgrounds in the same school due to limited local school options.

Our study looked at two schools that had mixed enrollments. One was a formally integrated school, in which the mixed enrollment was deliberate. The other was a circumstantially integrated school. It should also be pointed out that while integration in Northern Irish policy tends to focus on Catholics and Protestants; in reality, a surge of immigration from Eastern Europe, Western Asia, and Africa has dramatically altered the nature of cultural diversity in Northern Ireland generally and its schools specifically. Both of the schools in our study included a significant number of recent immigrants from a wide range of cultures. Meadow School and Mountain School (we used pseudonyms) were respectively the integrated school, and the circumstantially-mixed school.

Meadow School and Mountain School offer a striking contrast with respect to school culture. While both were deliberate and consistent in the ways they managed student diversity, their approaches were very different. At Meadow School, student diversity was openly acknowledged, celebrated, and explored as an aspect of the school's daily life. At Mountain School, an ethos of "respect for all" was dominant with limited acknowledgment of the particular religious and cultural identities represented by the students. These patterns emerged clearly and consistently from interviews, observation, focus groups, and a review of school literature at each school.

At the time of the study, a visitor to Meadow School would enter through the front doorway into a large, well-lit reception area with sofas and a high ceiling. On the far wall, facing the main entrance were over 20 framed, poster-size, photo portraits of students. Under each portrait was a sign with the word 'Hello' in the home language of the student. The assemblage dominated the space and literally put a face on the rich student diversity of the school. Hallways and classrooms had boards hung on the walls that changed regularly, featuring images and information for religious festivals of different faiths. Assemblies were held periodically to introduce students and staff to a particular faith, followed by whole-school discussion.

At the time of the study, the school had recently begun a "language of the month" program, including an assembly, with students teaching their peers simple words and phrases. The whole school used the new words for greetings during that month. Assemblies were also held to recognize indigenous histories and culture. For example, assemblies were held for the Battle of the Boyne, and for the 1916 Easter Rising.

The cafeteria at Meadow School offered food that was halal, and, during Ramadan, a private space was set aside for Muslim students to pray and fast, if they chose, instead of going to the cafeteria. Clothing was modified for Muslim students in physical education, and, the principal reported, this accommodation was discussed with all the students. Newcomers (the term used for immigrants) at Meadow School began with a 12-week English intensive course while they attended 'practical' subjects such as PE, art, and home economics so that, according to the principal, "they are bonding with their peers and so that they are also being included as part of the school as early as possible and to try and alleviate a them-and-us type attitude." Classes during the first three years (8–10) at Meadow School were all mixed-ability classes. Newcomers, after their transition period, were fully integrated, and staff training was substantial for differentiation of instruction.

Meadow School administrators and staff reached out to the surrounding neighborhoods to engage various cultural communities. The principal described several related events, rendered below in her own words:

> So we had a [Meadow] in the community day where community leaders came to the school, and discussed with staff the challenges, the customs, the practices, the perception of the school, how there could be better relationships. And that allowed us to get maybe a deeper insight into how we could best fit the children. . . . And I think it has allowed some of our students to forge very positive relationships and to get rid of some of those stereotypical preconceptions that they may have had prior to actually having the physical experience of meeting people from the Roma community, from Somalia, from Syria and all of that.

At Meadow School, students were sometimes handed responsibility for addressing culture-related school issues. For example, in the United Kingdom it is customary to wear a poppy pin on the lapel in commemoration of Remembrance Day, marking the end of World War I. In Northern Ireland, this practice has become a sectarian symbol and a source of conflict. Several months before the research study, a group of students had asked if they could wear an Easter lily pin, a symbol of the 1916 Easter Rising, and, in Northern Ireland, a direct response by Irish nationalists to the British custom of the poppy pin. The principal directed the matter to student council for discussion with the head of the History department. Through discussion, the students determined that it would be fine for both symbols to be worn. Students then informed the principal that, in the principal's words:

> If there were any issues with parents, that the students' council and the student body in the school representing the students across all year groups and Key Stages [grade levels] were happy to chat to the parents. And we didn't have any phone calls from parents about that.

At Meadow School, the Protestant-Catholic divide was just one element of diversity. The inclusion of newcomers had, in recent years, gotten equal if not more attention from the staff. The principal stated, "So the focus for us is not just on the Catholic and Protestant students, although that's very important, but also the other number of students come from different countries."

Mountain School's treatment of student diversity was very different from Meadow School. At Mountain School, there was very little overt acknowledgement of the rich diversity within the school. While a large banner celebrating the school's participation in a Shared Education collaborative with other schools prominently decorated an exterior wall facing the parking lot, there was no visible acknowledgement of the diversity that existed inside of the school. The principal said, about the school's approach to diversity, "it's not overt. It's not something that you shout about from the rooftops." Instead, he offered, the school insists simply on respect for all, regardless of background. He stated: "So all those kinds of messages are continually drummed into everyone about community. We're a family, we look out for each other, we look after each other, irrelevant of where you're from, your faith." The school's ethos of care and compassion was evident across staff interviews.

The principal spoke repeatedly of the "natural" approach the school takes toward diversity. As an example, he offered the story of a recent carnival held by the school as a fundraiser. At the carnival, several parents from the Polish community offered food items that were traditional.

> Three of the mums did a cake [table], and all the stuff was Polish. Now, no one overtly went to them and said, 'It would be a really good idea if the Polish community was all represented. Can you go and do this? It happened naturally, and I think that's part of the key in the school, that those parents feel part of the community, that they don't feel like they're treated any different. So there, it's not like their things are dismissed, and it's not like you push them away and hide them, but you also don't rush out.

As in Meadow School, the inclusion of newcomers loomed large as an element of the school's diversity. Along with the challenges to staff of incorporating English instruction for newcomers into the curriculum, the principal saw significant benefit to their membership in the school community. He commented:

> I think the fact that there was the Protestant, Catholic kind of . . . it's not an issue, but not an issue in this school, obviously, it's helped when we've started to get newcomers in. Because no one really bats an eyelid, culturally, it's not . . . they're very accepting. It helps with the respect for all and whatever your color, creed, background, gender, faith, makes no odds in the school.

Despite the presence of many nationalities and faiths, the school overall remained mostly silent on the subject. The school's website made no mention of the school's uniquely diverse demographics, instead repeating the more general respect-for-all message invoked by the staff. According to the website, the school focuses on "developing an atmosphere of mutual respect and caring."

In Meadow School, students overwhelmingly endorsed the multi-cultural nature of their school. One student remarked, "It's pretty straightforward. I mean, if there's people from different cultures, you're obviously going to be able to learn about their cultures more than you would otherwise." Most students went further, embracing the very deliberate way that Meadow School fostered cross-cultural understanding. A student remarked:

> You can't just put two people who don't know anything about the other person's religion, because we grew up in a society that puts stereotypes, and most of the time the stereotypes aren't true, but that's what we grew up with, so that's what we know. So then, if you put them in a room, then they're gonna get based off of those stereotypes, even though they might not be true. So then I think it's better for people like explain, like, 'This isn't true. This is actually how it is,' so they can be more understanding.

At Mountain School, student feelings about their school's multi-cultural make up were mixed. While some students endorsed it, others expressed hesitation. For example, one student remarked:

> I think that it helps you in some aspects, but then other aspects it sort of holds you back cause there's a lot of fights and stuff, mainly between people from different nationalities and stuff in school. People from our nationality. . . . I think the majority of fights is between both nationalities. The help is in the way they help us understand their background and where they come from, but then sometimes it leads to conflict, just because two sides don't agree.

Another student remarked about the number of cultures represented in the school, "Yeah. It's too many. Like you just can't get to socialize with everyone cause there's different people." While extreme comments were rare, one student remarked, "It's lies. Learn more from more cultures. . . . I didn't always go to this school. I went to a very conservative, Christian school before and I learnt a lot more about all the cultures and stuff like that there."

At Meadow School, students tended to see multiculturalism enriching the academic experience, while at Mountain School, it was seen sometimes as an impediment. A Meadow School student remarked:

> When I was doing my GCSE testing in maths, there's the teacher talking about the subject, and I was like, 'I really don't know what's going on,' and then one of our Romanian students was giving an example of how they were helping build a hut for refugees, and they had to build a certain amount of things, and I was like, 'Oh, I actually get that now.'

At Mountain School, students sometimes saw their school's multiculturalism as a barrier to academics. One student exchange went as follows:

GIRL: I think the teachers spend more time focusing on the people from the different cultures and you don't get the—
BOY: Correct amount of time—
GIRL: Yeah. So that's . . . they're focusing more on them and trying to educate them rather than—
BOY: Us—

The two schools also differed in the patterns of voluntary cross-cultural mixing reported by students. At Meadow School, students indicated it was quite normal for students to mix across culture groups. The following exchange is representative.

INTERV: So do any of you, or do any of the people you know, have a friend who's from a different cultural background and you see each other outside of school?
GIRL 1: Me, all of us.
GIRL 2: We all do.
INTERV: So that wouldn't be odd to go shopping together, or go to each other's house?
GIRL 1: We're just all the same. We don't really take into consideration what difference the other person is.
INTERV: Okay. Alright, I'm seeing lots of nodding heads around the table, I guess the general experience here.

At Mountain School, attitudes reported by students tended toward tolerance of other groups that often stopped short of friendship. One student commented:

> You get along with people in your class 'cause they're in your class, you can't do nothing about that, you're not going to be so hard on them, but you do see groups in our school, like people from their own religion or culture, like in groups, but it's not in a bad way. If you walked past them and you want to have a conversation with them, they're not going to be like 'What are you doing? Go away.' They'll have a conversation with you. Obviously, they're just comfortable with the people that they know and the people they know partially and get along with.

In Meadow School, deliberate attention to diversity created an all-school 'meta-curriculum' consisting of assemblies, all-school discussions, classroom rituals, school-wide problem solving, thoughtful interventions, and community outreach. This meta-curriculum was an important form of instruction for students not formally acknowledged through assessment schemes or course designs. The instructional demand of this meta-curriculum was real, and student learning with respect to intellectual openness, collaboration, and problem solving was apparent for students of all ages and cultural backgrounds.

At the heart of integrated schooling in Northern Ireland is the belief that face-to-face contact between members of rival groups can improve intergroup relations. Known as "contact theory"[1] proposed by Gordon Allport in 1954, a recent meta-analysis provides powerful confirmation.[2] The difference in openness to cultural diversity displayed by students at Meadow School and Mountain School is consistent with findings elsewhere concerning multicultural education, suggesting that a 'color-blind' approach, apparent in Mountain School, is not effective in building understanding and empathy across cultural difference.[3] While Mountain School principal and staff displayed a genuine attitude of caring toward their students it was not sufficient to build trust among groups and exploit cultural diversity as a learning resource. In contrast, Meadow School's very deliberate approach to raising up student identities and cultural diversity allowed students to learn from their diverse backgrounds and promoted positive outlooks toward other cultures specifically and pluralism generally.

Is this relevant to the United States? A great deal of it, yes. First, however, it is important to acknowledge that Northern Ireland and the United States represent distinctly different contexts with respect to history and culture. In the United States, white society is economically and cultural dominant, while Catholics and Protestants in Northern Ireland have achieved rough parity. Catholics and Protestants together, however, constitute a white,

English-speaking majority, dominant over many recent immigrant groups. Acknowledging differences in context, there is still much that can be learned. Northern Ireland's experiment with integration demonstrates that deliberate mixing of students from distinct cultural backgrounds, coupled with a schoolwide commitment to the exploration and celebration of diversity, combined with a focus on student identity development, can powerfully influence student attitudes, their engagement with school, and possibly their academic achievement. These findings closely match research focused on racially integrated schools in the United States.[4] In both instances, an emphasis on psychological safety, as we observed among outstanding teachers in our own studies, is crucial. Despite these findings, schools and communities in the United States continue to resist integration. Evidence suggests school segregation is on the rise nationally.[5] If we are going to benefit from the cultural diversity of American society, we need to commit to engagement across cultures. School is an excellent place to do the work.

Notes

1. Allport, G. W. (1954). *The Nature of Prejudice*. Reading, MA: Addison-Wesley.
2. Pettigrew, T., & Tropp, L. (2006). A meta-analytic test of inter-group contact theory. *Journal of Personality and Social Psychology, 90*(5), 751–783. doi:10.1037/00223514.90.5.751
3. Several works relevant to multicultural education are as follows:

    Banks, J. A., & McGee, C. (2015). *Multicultural Education: Issues and Perspectives* (9th ed.). Hoboken, NJ: Wiley.
    Carr, L. G. (1997). *"Color-Blind" Racism*. Thousand Oaks, CA: Sage Publications.
    McGlynn, C. (2011). Negotiating difference in post-conflict Northern Ireland: An analysis of approaches to Integrated Education. *Multicultural Perspectives, 13*(1), 16–22. doi:10.1080/15210960.2011.548179
    Moncada Linares, S. (2016). Othering: Towards a critical cultural awareness in the language classroom. *HOW, 23*(1), 129–146. doi:10.19183/how.23.1.157

4. See, for example, Hawley, W. D. (2007). Designing schools that use student diversity to enhance learning of all students. In E. Frankenberg & G. Orfield (Eds.), *Lessons in Integration: Realizing the Promise of Racial Diversity in American Schools* (pp. 31–56). Charlottesville: University of Virginia Press.
5. Stancil, W. (2018, March 14). School segregation is not a myth. *The Atlantic*. www.theatlantic.com/education/archive/2018/03/school-segregation-is-not-a-myth/555614/

7 Assessment

Schooling in our era will be remembered, in part, for testing, and the general dismay surrounding it. In many places, students sit for exams repeatedly through the year while instruction focuses on prep for the next test, never more than a few weeks away. Many parents have grown frustrated, some choosing to *opt out* of exams altogether.[1] A school board member from Quincy, Massachusetts, sums it up: "The school year has become one long period of diffusion and cram, the object of which is to successfully pass a stated series of examinations. This leads directly to superficiality. Smatter is the order of the day."[2] This comment captures our contemporary problem. But what's striking about it, besides, maybe, the delightful word, "smatter," is that it comes from an article written in 1879. Allow us a short historical detour to make a point.

Charles Adams, at the time, head of the Quincy School Board, was frustrated by the examination system in use by the schools in which students simply parroted the facts introduced in class. Mr. Adams, like many in our own times, wanted more. His frustration, shared by other board members, led to the hiring of a charismatic superintendent of schools who focused on deeper learning through a more interactive approach to instruction and assessment. The new superintendent, Francis W. Parker, shortly became famous for "the Quincy Method." Visitors flocked to the Quincy schools; laudatory articles were published in prominent journals. But then critics started to speak up, partially misrepresenting the facts, as is often the case. They argued that eliminating books deprived children of the accumulated wisdom of the ages and that a purely "oral method" was no substitute. Parker, however, was not advocating for the elimination of books nor a purely "oral" method. Rather, he favored library books that children would choose themselves, over textbooks, thereby heightening student engagement. After five years, Superintendent Parker left Quincy. With time, his innovations faded, and the conventional approach to teaching and exams resumed.[3]

We share this historical nugget for two reasons. First, it makes the point in a short space that the battles over instruction and assessment so familiar today are not unique to our times. They've been fought before. In fact, they represent perennial tensions that play out in semi-predictable ways—patterns from which we can learn a great deal. Second, this short episode underscores the power of the aphorism *assessment drives instruction*. If we change the ways we assess student learning, we insert a powerful lever under the whole system that can upend it—as Francis Parker did in Quincy long ago.

In this chapter, we explore assessment as an important system-level support, a powerful lever, for changes to instruction. Thoughtfully deployed it will foster excellence; implemented sloppily, or for the wrong reasons, it can drive an entire system toward superficiality and, well, smatter. We begin with the essential backstory to our current assessment plight, highlight perennial tensions of assessment systems and the political activity that determines their fate. Describing just a few crucial moments from recent policy history, we will see how our current focus on large-scale, test-driven assessment came to be and what we can do about it. We do not aspire to offer a comprehensive history in this short space.[4] Instead, we provide the details of several crucial policy turns. We then offer an overview of the technical features of various approaches to assessment and their implications for learning, and we discuss the problematic nature of testing for civil rights work. Next, we pivot again to Northern Ireland. We use the school system there as a case study to illuminate tensions around assessment and cultural difference experienced in both societies. We conclude with a look at the current state of assessment policy in the United States. We offer recommendations, based on historical patterns and contemporary research. We conclude with some inspiring examples of assessment policy work, currently under way, that support excellence *redefined*.

Accountability, the Backstory

On a windy day in May of 1964, Lyndon Johnson delivered the commencement address at the University of Michigan at Ann Arbor.[5] The speech signaled themes of a policy, still in formation, which was to guide Johnson in his presidency after the 1964 election. To the new graduates, he said, ". . . in your time, we have the opportunity to move not only toward the rich society and the powerful society, but upward to the great society." This "great society," he said later in the speech, "demands an end to poverty and racial injustice." Education, in Johnson's view, was the engine that would drive out poverty. He said, "Poverty must not be a bar to learning, and learning must offer an escape from poverty." In a series of domestic programs that followed, known as the Great Society, opportunity was the driving logic. Given the opportunity, the argument went, people would naturally seek advancement. And the cornerstone was education.

Public awareness of social inequality had been recently heightened with the publication of Michael Harrington's influential *The Other America* (1962),[6] which claimed that the image of American affluence cultivated during the Eisenhower years masked an invisible "Other America" in which 40 to 50 million Americans lived in material poverty. James Conant's equally influential *Slums and Suburbs: A Commentary on Schools in Metropolitan areas*, published in 1961, exposed similarly stark inequality in America's public schools, though with a very different analysis.[7] The public was primed to embrace a remedy based on the idea of *opportunity* with a focus on the nation's schools.

Less than a year after Johnson's "Great Society" speech, as it later became known, Congress passed, and the freshly-elected President signed, the Elementary and Secondary Education Act of 1965. The new law injected millions of federal dollars into schools and school systems across the country. The law stated,

> In recognition of the special educational needs of children of low-income families and the impact that concentrations of low-income families have on the ability of local educational agencies to support adequate educational programs, the Congress hereby declares it to be the policy of the United States to provide financial assistance (as set forth in this title) to local educational agencies serving areas with concentrations of children from low-income families to expand and improve their educational programs.[8]

Though the law required annual testing,[9] there were no stakes explicitly associated with test results. The logic of the law was simple: provide opportunity, mitigate the material impact of poverty on children, and achievement would rise.

And achievement did rise, modestly. An analysis carried out by Linda Darling Hammond, based on a variety of measures, demonstrates that the Great Society investment in public schools paid off as the achievement gap between blacks, whites, and Hispanics, began to narrow.[10] This happened in the absence of high-stakes tests, and in the absence of the 'results'-based accountability measures lowered upon schools in the No Child Left Behind era. But we're getting ahead of our story.

Even as Johnson's Great Society was building a new federal policy architecture, there were strong ideological counter currents eroding its base. Johnson's view and the majority view of the Democrat-controlled Congress at the time was sharply at odds with the conservative vision. Democrats favored a communitarian, social reformist ethic, to be advanced by the federal government. Republicans, skeptical of what they saw as social engineering by the state, costly expansion of the federal government, inefficiency inherent in state run programs, and a threat to local autonomy, kept a steady drumbeat for their alternate views through the Johnson years. Then, conservative values gained ascendancy in the 1980s under President Ronald Reagan. A host of federal programs targeting inequality experienced sharp reductions in funding or elimination.[11]

Democrat and Republican values, on display in the see-sawing treatment of federal investment in education, were sharply at odds. Which is why a compromise policy stance advanced by Bill Clinton in the 1990s found an audience and set the stage for change. Clinton advocated a "Third Way," part of a larger, international movement of the same name that sought a reconciliation of old-Left and traditional conservative ideas about economics and the state. For Clinton's policy agenda, the reconciliation meant investment by the federal government in domestic programs long supported by Democrats but with the requirement, demanded by conservatives, that programs must show results—return on investment. If they can't show results, then they should be cut. For Clinton's Third Way to work, targets had to be set and instruments created to measure outcomes. Thus was born the standards-and-testing movement that has so influenced contemporary education. Clinton's Third Way took root during his eight years in office, but it was not until a Republican once again took up residence in the White House that a grand compromise was reached between liberals and conservatives with respect to the federal role in education. This compromise came to fruition in the 2002 re-authorization of ESEA known as No Child Left Behind (NCLB), under George W. Bush. NCLB required states to set learning standards and test every child in a public school on a regular basis, which meant once a year in grades 3 through 8 and once again in high school. In exchange for this new requirement, insisted upon by conservatives, new federal dollars would flow into education, targeting especially needy students, schools and districts, as many Democrats wanted. Rewards and sanctions were attached to test results. The funding was real, and the stakes were high.

As the standards movement advanced, the education sector saw the rise of several competing conceptions of the assessment that would accompany the standards. During the 1980s and 1990s, three camps formed: a student-centered camp, a subject-centered camp, and an accountability camp. Student-centered educators were accustomed to performative assessments—projects, portfolios, juried exhibitions—that displayed complex skills and dispositions in the context of real-world learning. Meanwhile, subject-centered educators leaned more heavily on term papers, labs, math proofs, and other traditional exercises that also demanded complex thought. E.D. Hirsch and his Core Knowledge Foundation, like Sizer's and Meier's Coalition, rallied hundreds of schools to its cause.[12] Meanwhile, the accountability camp focused heavily on selected response tests because they had the aura, if not the substance, of reliability and validity. The accountability camp was centered not in schools but departments of education (federal and state) and conservative think tanks. Advocates included Diane Ravitch, Chester Finn, and organizations such as the Hoover Institution and the Thomas B. Fordham Institute.[13] As pressure for accountability increased within the public arena, portfolios, juried exhibitions, term papers, math proofs, and labs were pushed to the margins. Selected response, standardized exams met the accountability demands of the system, and soon dominated the life of public schools. Long standing, high quality assessment practices fell away, sharply eroding the quality of teaching and learning in schools and classrooms. And for schools and classrooms lacking strong assessment practices, the new metrics began to shape an educational experience unworthy of aspiration.

To summarize: In the space of 40 years, we saw several significant developments: 1) Scale: growth in the federal government's role in education meant an enormous leap in the scale of the education system. The activity in individual classrooms, virtually every classroom, was governed directly by federal law. The system applied pressure for tighter coupling among its layers: classroom, school, locality, state, and federal government. Players within the system, however, resisted. 2) Standards: The federal government started with a focus on school inputs in order to create opportunity and ended with a focus on outputs in the name of results. 3) Standardized tests: Selected response, large scale exams became the *sine qua non* of student assessment. 4) Stakes: Test results were used to reward and punish teachers and schools. The interaction of these elements have defined the role of assessment in our times and have powerfully re-shaped the nature of teaching and learning in our public schools. While policy *talk* has ranged widely, policy *action* in recent decades has focused on measurement using selected response items for purpose of accountability-of-results with high stakes attached. To understand important nuances of accountability, we look next at the purpose and various forms of assessment.

Assessment: A Primer

The challenge of assessment in our time boils down to three considerations: priority, approach, and purpose. Measurement and complexity constitute competing *priorities*. Selected response and constructed response are two *approaches* to assessment. Finally, learning and accountability are, broadly speaking, two *purposes* to which assessment may be set. First, let's take a look at measurement and complexity.

Priority: Measurement vs. Complexity

There is an inverse relationship between complexity of task and ease of measurement. The more complex a task, the harder it is to measure. The simpler a task, the easier it is to measure. Imagine a high school that requires each of its students to complete a 'senior project.' It is a year-long undertaking that involves the identification of a question, related research, the development of a product, an internship or other extended engagement with the adult world of work, and a final presentation before a panel of community members. Each element is assessed with a rubric and the rubrics are keyed to learning outcomes required for graduation. Measuring the degree to which a student has met the outcomes and whether a student is therefore ready to graduate is an extremely complex and recursive undertaking. To reduce the assessment of this complex undertaking to a number on a line with technically sound validity and reliability would be extremely difficult. Now imagine another school, in which students must take and pass a standardized test of reading and math in order to graduate—an 'exit exam.' The test consists of multiple-choice questions and several narrowly proscribed, short, written responses. If it is constructed with care, both validity and reliability can be readily established. But because of the nature of the test items, the complexity of tasks is necessarily limited. The task demand associated with the senior project is broad and deep. Task demand for the exit exam is narrow and shallow. Recall for a minute the taxonomy of deeper learning skills from Chapter One (Table 7.1):

Table 7.1 Taxonomy of Deeper Learning Skills

Cognitive Domain	Interpersonal Domain	Intrapersonal Domain
Recall	Teamwork/collaboration	Intellectual openness
Application	Leadership	Metacognition
Analysis		
Evaluation		
Creative thinking		

It is easy to imagine the senior project demanding of the student every skill in this taxonomy many times over in the course of the year. Next, consider the task demand associated with the test. It will likely hit the first two or three elements in the cognitive domain and little else. The sort of teaching required to prepare a student to succeed on the exam will likely consist of lots of memorization of facts and formulas, and drills. Consider, also, the crucial element of transfer. Ask yourself which experience is more likely to foster transfer of learning to new contexts: the year-long senior project, in which transfer is embedded, or the test-prep course that culminates in a selected response exam? A major problem of our time is the system's intense focus on measurement at the expense of task complexity. This leads to our second element of assessment: *approach.*

Approach: Selected Response vs. Constructed Response

There is a wide variety of assessment approaches in use in schools. There are on-demand traditional tests, portfolios, extended projects, juried exhibitions, thesis papers, lab reports, math proofs, original art, performances. In the world of psychometrics, all assessments can be placed in one of two categories: 1) selected response; and 2) constructed response. Assuming that any assessment is, to some degree, the student's response to a prompt, a student may *select* a response from a list or a student may *construct* a response from a blank page. A multiple-choice question is the classic selected response item. Virtually everything else is constructed. For purposes of measurement, selected response items offer the benefit of simple clarity. You are right, or you are wrong. Which is why, if our priority is ease of measurement, selected response items are much preferred. Once we shift to constructed response, measurement is complicated by the fact that no longer is there an indisputably right answer. The construction, even, of a single word raises questions. *Does spelling count? If so, how much?* The more the student constructs, the more bedeviling is the task of measurement. If accuracy of measurement is the priority, and constructed response items are the approach, the prompt must be tightly constructed ("in an essay of five paragraphs . . . provide three examples . . . refer to two supporting documents . . . provide two quotations.") and the scoring rubric will be highly detailed, corresponding with the specifications of the prompt. Under these circumstances, the tasks for the student and the teacher quickly become less about demonstrating complex skills and more about compliance with complex regulations. This dynamic contributes to the "more steps" phenomenon found in our study of high- performing schools, but it does little to advance learning.

On the other hand, if complex task demand is the priority, then meeting the psychometric standards of reliability and validity will become more difficult. That's because constructed responses introduce judgment into the assessment process. Judgment is the semi-intuitive weighing of attributes not easily subject to measurement. The attributes in a highly developed, constructed response, such as a performance, are numerous, complex, and interactive. Consider diving. Olympic diving is judged for execution and degree of difficulty. Execution is divided into *approach, take-off, elevation, execution* and *entry*. Here is a description of just one of those elements: "Execution: The dive's components—straight, tuck, pike or free positions—must be performed crisply, with flair and control, and held long enough in flight to clearly identify them. A judge watches for proper mechanical performance, technique, form and grace."[14] Attributes such as *crispness, flair, control*, and *grace* are difficult to define, much less measure. The opportunity to observe them lasts maybe ten seconds. Therefore, instead of measurement, diving relies on judges—people who are expert in the field. The introduction of judgment into the assessment process raises a threat to reliability and validity. If judgment is semi-intuitive, it cannot be fully explained. It is to some extent, mysterious. Measurement experts do not like mystery. So when judgment is required by the nature of the task, special steps must be taken to mediate the threat of mystery. Judges will practice scoring with other judges, discuss their decisions, and norm their assessments. While this process will likely not result in the level of reliability and validity from a good, selected response test item, it helps narrow the gap. And it allows divers at the Olympics to show off their skills by diving, instead of sitting for an exam.

In the world of schools, where portfolios, performances, and juried exhibitions are sometimes used to assess complex skills, some combination of measurement and judgment is inevitable. To build reliability and validity without compromising task complexity, standards may be set, rubrics developed, and rater responses normed. Doing so is the necessary balancing act between the demands for credible standards of measurement and the teaching of complex skills. Doing it well is the challenging and messy work that responsible educators may not evade.

One other threat to measurement validity merits our consideration. Picture the classic 'final exam.' Row upon row of students seated at individual desks brought to the gymnasium for the final week of school. It's June and the gym is hot. Big, oscillating fans push warm air across the room. Backpacks are lined up against the wall and only a pencil and eraser may accompany the student to her desk. Instructions are given, and, on the head proctor's signal, students begin work. Time is limited, maybe three hours, no more. This elaborate, familiar ritual is intended to ensure that the results of the test represent the work of the student alone, without the assistance of any resources other than her own mind—maybe a calculator. If Mom has been helping with homework or if a sympathetic teacher has been providing a little more than coaching and guidance, it will show up on the test, where the training wheels are off.

The 'final exam' shows what an individual, without any resources, can do on demand, under pressure of high stakes and limited time. As with everything else we've discussed, this valuing of accurate measurement is a trade-off. While it's a great way to see what a person can do under a certain kind of pressure, it does not show us what a student is capable of accomplishing over time, with resources available, in collaboration with others—which is how most of the work of the world gets done. If, however, we choose a form of assessment that does not isolate the student in this way, how do we know what exactly the *student* has contributed to a piece of work as opposed to say, her teacher, parents, or classmates. Various approaches are taken to address this problem. In the United Kingdom, for example, students in a studio art class will be given a week to create art in response to a series of prompts. All their work must be done in class and all their materials must remain there. A teacher monitors the week-long undertaking. This is called 'controlled assessment' in the British system. It is used as an alternative to selected response exams when greater task complexity is the priority.[15] A related approach is sometimes used in connection with portfolios, where the student may be required to make a culminating oral presentation, discussing and reflecting on the material in the portfolio. The presentation is a check on the student's degree of agency and autonomy with the work in the portfolio. Can she discuss it ably? Does her commentary corroborate the skills the portfolio is intended to certify? And this leads us to our third consideration: *purpose*.

Purpose: Learning vs. Accountability

Broadly speaking, assessment may be set to two different purposes: learning and accountability. When the focus is learning, assessment becomes a tool to assist the growth and development of the student. Assessment may help diagnose a student's strengths and needs. What is the student good at, what does she understand? Where are the gaps, what does she need to work on? This will guide next steps in the instructional process. Assessment may also be used to certify when a student is ready to move to the next formal stage, be it 9th grade, college, or calculus. Some people refer to this distinction as formative and summative. We prefer the terms diagnose and certify because they make the purpose explicit.

Assessment may also be used to hold persons and institutions to account. What do the student, the teacher, the principal, or the school have to show for the investment of time, money, and other resources by the public? Accountability may focus on inputs, or it may focus on outcomes. The original ESEA, in 1964, required schools and states to account for appropriate distribution of funds, a kind of input. Other inputs might be class size, availability of free breakfast or lunch, disability access for the school building. Alternately, accountability may focus on outcomes: what percentage of students enrolled in ninth grade graduate within five years, what scores do students achieve on standardized tests? Often, stakes are associated with accountability. Sometimes, the stakes are dire: fines or criminal charges for misappropriation of funds. School closure for persistently low scores on exams.

Accountability also demands comparability. What can one school show for the investment of public dollars *compared to* another. Comparability is a useful quality, but, like so much else, it forces a trade-off. For assessments to be comparable, there must be some degree of standardization. Typically, standardizing is a top-down process. System leaders create assessments. School level educators and their students must comply. The trade-off is that systems rooted in compliance tend to be low performing (as we will see in the next chapter), compared with systems in which school level educators exercise professional judgment. Thus, standardization produces comparability, but it also produces mediocrity. Standardizing also disregards the fact that communities and individual students differ. Senior projects in a rural school may build the same skills as senior projects in a city school, but the questions, products, and internships will be widely different.

What is the perceived benefit of comparability? Rating schools better and worse opens the possibility of studying the practices at the *better* schools and applying them elsewhere. This sounds both logical and beneficial to the system as a whole. But the idea quickly becomes complicated. Research into organizational change has shown again and again that complex systems are not moved by mechanistic efforts at change that ignore beliefs, values, and deeply embedded institutional routines—the essence of culture. For example, in 2007, the Lawrence (Massachusetts) public schools undertook construction of a new high school campus consisting of six, autonomous small schools to replace the single comprehensive high school of 3000+ students. The dramatic architectural change reflected a vision rooted in recent educational research touting the benefits of small schools. There was a national 'small schools' movement fueled by over three billion dollars from the Federal Government's Small Schools program and the Bill and Melinda Gates Foundation.[16] Initially, in Lawrence, separate 'academies' were established, in the brand-new, completely separate buildings. But they were not granted the autonomy of a free-standing school. Erosion of what freedom they possessed began almost immediately as the underlying and unchanged culture of a comprehensive high school (think course electives, tracking, interlocking schedule, bells) asserted itself. Ten years later, the high school, in spite of its architecture, was again a comprehensive high school with the principal proudly announcing in his annual welcome-back letter to parents, the "alignment of the bell schedule from grades 9–12."[17] Leaders in Lawrence believed that changing the arrangement of the bricks would force a change in behavior. But mechanistic changes that ignore culture always fail. Applying 'best' practices elsewhere is far more complicated than it appears.

Another common feature of accountability is the deliberate exclusion of human judgment, especially by teachers, from the assessment process. Since the purpose is, in part, to judge teacher performance in order to apply rewards and sanctions, others are called on to conduct assessment. And, because the mysterious nature of human judgment threatens reliability, judgement is eliminated with selected-response items or minimized with tightly scripted, constructed-response items. As with other features of accountability, we can see here how its requirements present a trade-off with teaching and learning. A teacher knows her students' strengths and limitations best and is in the best position to assess their work. A teacher can use her own formal and informal assessments directly and continuously to inform instruction. But if teacher performance is being measured by student performance, the teacher must be excluded from the process.

Accountability and Social Justice

For all its flaws, the NCLB architecture of mandatory standardized tests for all, with public access to results, including disaggregation by sub-groups, produced valuable data to support civil rights work. The data provided undeniable empirical evidence to prosecute gaps in achievement. Many civil rights organizations initially cheered the new law. At the same time, the pressure for test performance created by NCLB, pushed teachers to focus on tested material and a 'test-prep' approach featuring low-level skills, such as recall and procedural thinking. Deeper learning skills that set future employees apart and make them much more employable and skills that foster strong identity development available easily to white people, were denied to people of color. Demands to close achievement gaps in schools serving high need communities intensified these practices. While NCLB's simple logic of accountability, reward, and sanction promised to close gaps, the result was quite likely a widening of gaps with respect to the deeper learning skills for which there are no large-scale metrics.[18] Civil rights leaders that heralded passage of NCLB, later condemned its design and outcomes.[19]

The forms and purposes of assessment are complex. To see how the dynamics play out in schools, we turn once again to Northern Ireland and another study from our series that helps us understand our own society by revealing similar dynamics in a society just different enough to illuminate important themes affecting both.

For this study, we ventured into Northern Irish schools that, like the American schools in one of our earlier studies, were highly successful with state tests while also showing promise in the teaching of 21st century skills. We spent time in four schools, each of which served a significant number of students from low-income families. We visited classes, interviewed teachers, administrators, and students, and spent time in the faculty room, corridors, cafeteria, and playground. For our purposes here, we share what we found with respect to assessment.

Our analysis revealed that the variety of assessment strategies roughly corresponded with the presence and absence of deeper learning skills instruction from classroom to classroom. The assessment approach associated with any course strongly influenced students' exposure to complex tasks. We found a variety of strategies were used to assess student learning—depending on the subject, academic track, and grade level. Strategies included externally administered, traditional exams (time-bound, on demand); locally developed exams (also on-demand and time-bound); performances and projects accompanied by rubrics and often collected into a portfolio; practical exams; and a mix of familiar and variously defined teacher-developed assessments such as daily homework, participation, quizzes, essays, labs, problem sets, etc.

In general, we observed that as reliance on performances, projects, and portfolios increased, so too did the instructional demand for deeper learning skills. Inversely, as reliance on an externally administered traditional exam increased, instructional demand for deeper learning skills decreased. In learning situations where teacher-developed assessment strategies were used and in situations where there was *no* formal assessment, the instructional demand for deeper learning skills also tended to be strong. In what follows, we give a run-down of what happened instructionally in situations governed by different assessments. We should add that we've translated terms used in the Northern Ireland system to their American equivalent. For example, grades 6 through 8, in Northern Ireland are called Key Stage 3; courses taken by 11th- and 12th-graders heading to college are called 'A-level.'

Instruction emphasizing deeper learning skills was evident in courses in which assessment was something other than a traditional external exam, meaning a written, on-demand, time-bound test. Such courses tended to include classes in the lower grades in which students do not take system exams: grade 9 and 10 courses with less than 50% exam assessment, and 11th- and 12th-grade courses with less than 50% exam assessment. Deeper learning skill instruction was especially evident in courses driven by an assessed project with a product, meaning an extended, complex task, contextualized by a real-world scenario, culminating either in a performance or a product or both.

For example, in a science class from Key Stage 3 (6th grade to 8th grade), students were asked to work in pairs to create several different ratios of ingredients in a set of test tubes to produce solutions with various pH levels. The task required students to think like scientists, thereby using strategic reasoning in order to make sense of the phenomenon they observed. Indeed, the teacher set before students a task that required them to demonstrate their ability to apply major aspects of scientific investigation, namely, collecting data through observation, questioning and hypothesizing about what they observed, and testing and evaluating their hypothesis. Moreover, the collaborative nature of the task meant that students served as a resource for learning—potentially expanding the pool of knowledge students have of the scientific principles that underlie pH levels. The collaborative nature of the task also necessarily meant that students had to practice interpersonal skills (e.g., effectively communicating, cooperating) in order to produce solutions with various pH levels. By exposing students to a task with inherently high cognitive and interpersonal demand and with application to the worlds of medicine, oceanography, forestry, food science, water treatment, etc., the teacher provided opportunities for deeper learning. In this class, there was no external exam.

As students move from the grade 6–8 sequence to 9–10 sequence, assessment in many courses shifts to external examination. For science, most of the assessment in grades 9–10, measured as percentage of mark, is based on an external exam. Teachers commented frequently in focus groups that the shift in assessment from Key Stage 3 to Key Stage 4, across many subjects, produced a shift in teaching featuring a reduction in demand for deeper learning skills and an increase in demand for recall and application. One teacher commented, "In Key Stage 3 classes, all the wider skills [deeper learning] have been planned for, but at Key Stage 4, they're not. It's all tests." Another teacher during the same focus group said, "I find a gap between Key Stage 3 [and Key Stage 4]. The first [Key Stage 4] exam is very much about [recall, application, and analysis] skills. And there's so much to learn that it is incredibly content led." During another teacher focus group, a teacher commented:

> Our revised curriculum at Key Stage 3 is all about skills—managing your own learning, interpersonal skills—and we all assess those. But at Key Stage 4 they're not really in the exam papers. So it seems to be important at Key Stage 3 but it's not in there in Key Stage 4. There are gaps there.

Classroom observations and interview comments like these suggest that a reliance on external exams tends to reduce the level of demand when compared with courses that are not assessed with an external exam. And, while teacher comments could be interpreted as reinforcing critics' concern about a 'gap' between discipline-specific content and deeper learning (in applying discipline specific knowledge), the classroom instruction highlighted here suggests that addressing both is possible when the primary means of evaluating students' learning is not an external exam.

Not all 9–10 and 11–12 courses, however, are governed primarily by external exams. For example, in Engineering, only 40% is external exam.

Interestingly, the skill demand in such courses tended to be high. For example, in 10th-grade engineering, students were charged with the task of designing a table top holder for a tablet computer. Each student had to complete a series of technical drawings with extensive notes. They had to evaluate their drawings and, based on their knowledge of relevant engineering principles, they had to make reasoned decisions about which design to pursue. Moreover, the task required students to think creatively to design a holder that met the specifications—students had to engage in thoughtful planning in order to create a new structure. Following is an excerpt from research notes just as the teacher had finished giving an explanation of the task to the class.

> [S]tudents seem quite attentive and engaged. He tells the students to get started. As they start, students ask questions, which he fields while students are starting work. 9:42 All students appear to be at work. Some are at computers, others at table with pencils and drawings, one is consulting with teacher with a drawing in front of him. Some students are working quietly on their own. Others are chatting. Talk appears to be mostly about the work. There is an atmosphere that is purposeful but relaxed.

Importantly, the purposeful nature of the task suggests clear lesson intentionality and task accountability. In other words, it is clear to students what they are to produce, they are aware of the resources available to them (including their own notes and the teacher's feedback), and they know that they will be called on to demonstrate their knowledge and skill (when they present their final product). Such an open-ended, high-risk task that requires students to rely on their own creativity could produce anxiety and disengagement in students; often students respond to such task demands by trying to mediate the perceived risk. They do this by asking questions that will transform academically rigorous tasks (i.e., those that require higher level cognitive processes) into low-level procedural tasks.[20] In the class highlighted here, a student and teacher were observed in a short exchange:

STUDENT: Do I get marks for putting a label under the drawing? Do I get marks for putting a wee explanation over here?
TEACHER: You get marks for showing understanding of your design. You get marks for designing something that can actually be made.

While the student tries to mediate the risk associated with this task by trying to boil it down to something easier/more low level, the teacher redirects the student to his responsibility for designing (engineering) a table that can actually be used (i.e., will hold up a tablet). This is not to say that students in the class are not receiving the critical feedback they need from the teacher to execute the task. Rather, the teacher deflects low-level questions by offering feedback that is responsive to the technical and creative challenges inherent in the engineering task. Thus, the teacher mediates students' perception of risk and encourages their full engagement by creating a deeper learning environment characterized by clear purpose, personal responsibility, and support.

The example above represents, as well, another category of classes in which a project and a related product were the main object of student attention. The teacher's role in such classes was deliberately underplayed or backgrounded, while the student's role was foregrounded. The importance of the teacher's role was underscored in how the goals of the task are explained, in what resources the students had at their disposal during execution of the task (i.e., peers, teacher feedback, materials, exemplars, etc.), and in how students were asked to account for their learning once the task was executed. While the teacher orchestrated the classroom activity in his set up and monitoring, students were the primary actors during class: they are doing the work.

These examples are representative of consistent patterns observed across all of the schools we visited. A major challenge for secondary schools in Northern Ireland is finding ways to infuse higher level thinking into classes that are dominated by traditional, external exams. While teachers in 6th–8th-grade classes and 9th–10th-grade classes without a formal exam were able to bridge the ostensible gap between rigorous content and deeper learning skills, many 9th–10th-grade classes were dominated by teaching and learning that promotes recall and procedural application. Ironically, subjects viewed as core academic disciplines—science, math, history, English—tended to be governed by on-demand tests, pressuring teachers to focus on recall and procedural skills. At the same time, disciplines seen as marginal to academic life—drama, fine arts, engineering—tended to be governed by other kinds of assessment, for which instructional demand tended to be deeper and broader. One principal commented that when he was at university, he found that the few classmates of his who had come from vocational secondary schools were far better prepared for the demands of university learning than he, who came from an elite grammar school. He attributed this to the depth and breadth of task demands associated with vocational courses.

In Northern Ireland, the stakes associated with exam scores are at least as high as in the United States. Results of 'A-level' (grades 11–12) exams largely determine admission to universities. Results from the general certificate of secondary education (GCSE) exams at grade 10, influence school reputation, a critical feature in a region with a shrinking population of teenagers and declining secondary school enrollments. The test results also steer students toward a vocational track or a pre-university track.

We have not yet mentioned the feared 'transfer exam' taken by students at the end of 5th grade, the result of which determines whether a student will attend an elite high school ('grammar school') which nearly ensures passage to a university education, or a 'secondary school' from which university admission is far less certain. Because unemployment is high in Northern Ireland and because sectarian violence is heavily concentrated in the very divided, lower income neighborhoods of Belfast and other cities and towns, well-paying jobs are highly sought after. But they are not readily available and anything less will steer an individual toward both material want and dangerous, violent neighborhoods. Though educated families regularly complain about the test-obsessed system, they endure it because it so powerfully governs their children's fate in a society with seemingly limited access to peace and prosperity. Likewise, thoughtful school leaders long for a different approach to assessment but buckle down under extreme test pressure to save their schools from declining enrollment and the always looming spiral toward closure. The Department of Education abolished the transfer exam in 2008, but so intense is the competition among parents to secure a place in the elite grammar schools, that the schools, themselves, under parental pressure retained the test.

The patterns in Northern Ireland, are reflective of experience across the United Kingdom with a range of assessments at scale. Because accountability is king, any departure from the psychometric purity of on-demand tests and selected response test items is viewed with skepticism—just as in the United States, only more intensely. In 2016, the Head of England's exam system, Dennis Opposs, wrote a lengthy review of accountability there.[21] He made the point that non-exam assessments have faced an uphill battle for decades in a system driven by large-scale, high-stakes metrics. Various sorts of school-based projects, performances, portfolios and 'practicals' have been increasingly marginalized because of the potential 'threat' that teachers may provide assistance or apply unfair scoring. What Opposs does not acknowledge is that because the system is tilted so heavily in the direction of accountability, measurement is prioritized steeply over task complexity. In recent years, the percentage of GCSE and A-level scores derived from non-exam assessments has been sharply reduced, and, in some subjects, eliminated. Opposs, a defender of the system, offers an odd conclusion, suggesting that the range of complex skills covered by local, non-exam assessments, can now be taught more effectively because teachers are "freed from the need to carry out set piece practicals with the aim of maximizing marks." This, he concludes, "has allowed teachers to provide students with much better opportunities to develop their skills." Odd that a defender of measurement precision would advance a claim with little evidence for a skill set essential to work and civic life.

The nature of large-scale assessment in Northern Ireland, and the U.K. more generally, presents us with a cautionary tale, a possible—perhaps likely—scenario for the United States should we continue down the accountability path. Given growing income inequality in the United States, the stakes of educational achievement are growing as well. The differential futures dictated by success in school and its absence are increasingly stark: a path to relative prosperity and fulfillment on the one hand; unemployment, material want, violent neighborhoods on the other. In the mid-1960s, where this chapter began, growing signs of deep social inequality across the United States propelled Lyndon Johnson's Great Society policies. Today, the warning signs are far more dire: deeper economic inequality, mass incarceration, and declining social mobility. The Economic Policy Institute found in 2015 that the top 1% of American households "received, on average, 26.3 times as much income as a family in the bottom 99 percent," and that inequality, which had been growing steadily since 1973, had accelerated in the post-recession era, 2009–2018.[22] Meanwhile, the United States has the highest incarceration rate of any nation in the world.[23] Bear in mind, the list includes historically repressive societies, such as Cuba, Russia, and China. Add to these signs, the fact that income mobility in the United States has declined sharply in recent decades and the picture that emerges is a nation, for many, of sharply limited opportunity.[24] Depending on how we choose to proceed, our schools can serve as a powerful resource to combat social inequality or simply another institution that reproduces it.

A Better Path Forward

In 2016, President Obama signed into law the Every Student Succeeds Act, which re-authorized the 50-year-old Elementary and Secondary Education Act created under the Johnson administration in 1965. In the run-up to ESSA passage, the public made known their displeasure with the deleterious consequences of a testing obsession fostered by NCLB. In several states, parents chose for their children to *opt-out* from state tests, threatening states with the withholding of federal money if their test participation rate fell below 95%. School and state superintendents tried desperately to frighten parents into submission. Many parents refused. Their Congressional representatives took note. In the ESSA reauthorization of ESEA, a window was opened. The law included a provision for as many as seven states to be chosen to pilot assessment systems featuring measures other than traditional, on-demand tests. Educational leaders at the state level were suddenly in an "unlocked cage."[25] However, on April 2, 2018, the deadline for submission of pilot proposals, only Louisiana, Puerto Rico, and New Hampshire chose to venture forth into the wider world. Apparently, state level educators have grown fond of their cage. While Louisiana's and Puerto Rico's proposals are relatively modest in scope, New Hampshire, as if affirming the state motto, "Live Free or

Die," proposed a wholesale rewrite of accountability as we know it, and, along with it, the nested operations of the system's various levels.

New Hampshire chose a route based on portfolios and juried exhibitions, but the state, wisely, learned from similar state level attempts in the 1990s that began with great fanfare, then sputtered and failed partly because teachers were not adequately prepared. New Hampshire has committed resources to build teacher capacity. It also is placing a sharp focus on reliability, validity, and comparability in an effort to balance the demands of large-scale accountability with complex instructional demand. Before we dive into New Hampshire, however, we look first at Vermont in the 1990s: why it failed, and how New Hampshire could succeed.

Performance Assessment in Vermont in the 1990s

In December of 1989, the governors and White House aides who had orchestrated the historic education summit in Charlottesville, Virginia, were preparing a proposal on education standards to hand off to the President in time for his State of the Union address, just one month off. They invited oral and written input from the public, and over 200 educators and business leaders gave live testimony. Amidst much talk of rigor, standards, and tests, Vermont Education Commissioner Richard Mills struck a different note. "People have to feel a sense of passion," he said.[26] "Passion" turned out to be at the heart of an experiment Mills was launching in Vermont as the state attempted to replace standardized exams with portfolios. The scheme was wildly popular with teachers. In 1990, the first year, 90 schools wanted in, but the state could support only 48. A year later, students in 138 schools were eagerly filling their portfolios with original work.[27] Commissioner Mills, it appeared, was bringing passion to scale. Classrooms were alive with learning, teachers were engaged by their own professional development, and there was unprecedented collaboration among educators within and across schools and districts.

There was evidence of teaching focused on 'the basics' *coupled with* complex skills. For example, in math classes, students had to solve complex math problems embedded in real-world contexts, and then talk about their process. Here was attention to problem solving, mathematical communication, and transfer, all before the term, '21st century skills,' was in circulation.

Early reports were encouraging.[28] But there were skeptics, not only of Vermont's effort, but of the approach that Vermont represented, loosely identified as 'performance assessment,' which included such elements as portfolios and peer review—a system based on evidence *plus judgment*, driven principally by classroom teachers and grounded in the actual products of students. 'Accountability' was the emerging zeitgeist and, with it, demands for watertight reliability, validity, and comparability. As well, cost was a key factor as the U.S. Federal Government and states envisioned large-scale assessment. In short, there was political pressure for standardized, selected response exams that were easy to score, cheap to administer, with results that can be quickly plotted as numbers on a line.

It turned out the psychometric cracks reported in a 1992 study by Dan Koretz at the RAND Corporation, opened into fissures, as reported in a follow-up study by the same author in 1995.[29] The later study showed lack of reliability, and offered recommendations on how to further develop systems to address reliability issues. But critics seized on the critical aspects of the report to damn the whole notion of portfolios, thus clearing a path for traditional tests, scaled up for system accountability. The Vermont initiative was scuttled and Richard Mills left Vermont, taking a new job as Commissioner of Education for the State of New York. Still touting portfolios upon his arrival there, he shortly became a convert to multiple choice tests, proposing that they become a requirement for every student enrolled in a public school across the state. This dramatic conversion took just four months, suggesting, perhaps, just how powerful the interests behind testing and measurement were in determining education assessment practices.

Déjà Vu All Over Again?

As educators, most notably in New Hampshire, try, once again, to scale up portfolios, they must find that elusive point of balance between the measurement world's demands for reliability, and the educational imperative to teach for deeper learning. What may they learn from the last cycle of learning vs. measurement in educational assessment? Vermont, in the 1990s, did not recognize the scale of the capacity challenge at the local level. Instituting a performance-based assessment system was not simply a matter of learning to administer a different kind of assessment, nor was it even about norming assessments across large numbers of teachers and schools. It required a fundamental reboot of teaching and learning. Recall and application skills, sufficient for success with conventional exams, left students utterly at a loss to master complex tasks, like those required for the portfolios and related standards. Re-learning—what organizational analysts call 'capacity building'—at the local level is crucial. Equally important is some soul searching at the state level about just how high a bar is needed for reliability, validity, and comparability given measurement's tendency to dumb down teaching.[30]

Recommendations

We can teach simple stuff with accountability metrics that are flawless (valid, reliable, and comparable), or we can teach complex stuff and have messy metrics. We can't have both. History bears this out, and we are playing out the familiar see-saw right now with the tension between the testing legacy of NCLB and the testing backlash that has brought on assessment pilots under ESSA. As long as we insist on watertight metrics, focused on learning outcomes as our accountability driver, we will fail to prepare kids for work, civic engagement, or personal fulfillment. We need a recalibration of the purpose for assessment: back-off the obsession with accountability, throttle up learning. We need to stop asking so incessantly, "How do we measure X?" and ask, instead, "How do we inspire and engage children and youth?"

Also, we need to stop looking to a public agency as the main driver of excellence in schooling. The education sector, in recent decades, has come to rely on state education bureaucracies, originally designed to distribute resources and ensure that tax dollars were not being misappropriated, as the driver of great schools. This is oddly Soviet. We don't expect the FDA or the USDA to deliver a great steak. That's the job of the restaurant. The agencies simply, and crucially, ensure the meat is not tainted. Likewise, we shouldn't look to a department of education (federal or state) to produce a great school; that's the job of the principal and teachers working with their community. With state accountability hogging the road, many of the other more promising drivers of excellence are getting pushed to the shoulder. Accrediting organizations are in decline as state reporting mandates suck up all resources available for external review. The National Board for Professional Teaching Standards, the one professional standards board that appeared, at one point, to have some influence, is in financial decline. Meanwhile, choice schemes, such as public charter schools, vouchers, magnet schools, and mission-driven alternative schools, are either threatened by profiteering, tilted to benefit the privileged, or homogenized by regulatory mandates to erase their distinctive qualities.

Another part of the answer, which assessment experts have advocated for decades, is the use of multiple measures. Instead of a single test, taken at the end of the year for a particular subject that determines success or failure with rewards or punishments for students, teachers, and schools, we need multiple indicators of the many facets of teaching, learning, and schools, in order to make small adjustments and, when required, a massive overhaul. A physician does not rely solely on a thermometer to diagnose and prescribe. An array of indicators will triangulate a good diagnosis. The exemplary teachers in our studies did this in the isolation of their classrooms, both in

Massachusetts and Northern Ireland. There are hopeful signs in some quarters that systems are beginning to heed this advice. We close this chapter with a short summary of a very promising initiative, with the potential to influence state bureaucracies, that is imaginatively developing the use of multiple measures.

In 2013, Jack Schneider was an assistant professor at Holy Cross College in Worcester, Massachusetts. Jack lived with his wife and their young daughter in Somerville. Despite the long commute to Worcester, Jack and his wife chose to stay in Somerville, partly because they really liked what they saw in the local schools. So they were discouraged when the *Boston Globe* ran its annual schools score card, based mainly on test scores. The kid-friendly school where their daughter was headed was at the bottom of the list. Where in the *Globe*'s metrics, they wondered, was there any accounting of the other things that matter to a family deciding which school is best for their child? Jack engaged the designer of the *Globe*'s scorecard in a conversation and soon they were working together to design a better approach. Jack, trained as an education historian, suddenly found himself on a personal quest for school quality measures that quickly mushroomed into a grant funded project involving numerous prominent school districts across Massachusetts—with the endorsement of the teachers' unions. Clearly, he had tapped into a rich vein of public interest. The Massachusetts Consortium for Innovative Education Assessment is developing an array of input and outcome measures for school quality, "built around multiple measures, which include academic, social-emotional, and school culture indicators, in order to piece together a fairer and more comprehensive picture of school performance."[31] The MCIEA is a wonderful example of what can be accomplished at a high level with a simple shift in focus. How to propel like-minded work across systems is the focus of the final chapter.

Notes

1. In New York State, for example, 20% of eligible test takers opted out in 2015, based on New York State Department of Education Reporting. New York State Education Department. (2015, August 12). [Press Release] *State Education Department Releases Spring 2015 Grades 3–8 Assessment Results*. Albany, NY: Author. Accessed 2/22/19: www.nysed.gov/news/2015/state-education-department-releases-spring-2015-grades-3-8-assessment-results
2. "The New Education in the Public Schools of Quincy, Mass." (1879) from Adams, C. F. (1879). *The New Departure in the Common Schools of Quincy*. Boston, 33–40 in Cohen, Sol, *Education in the United States: A Documentary History*. Random House, 1974, Vol. 3, 1811.
3. For more on Francis W. Parker, see Campbell, J. (1965). *The Children's Crusader: Colonel Francis W. Parker*. New York: Teachers College Press. Also, Katz, M. (1987). *Reconstructing American Education*. Cambridge, MA: Harvard

University Press. Also, Nehring, J. (2009). *The Practice of School Reform: Lessons from Two Centuries*. Albany, NY: SUNY Press.

4. For an excellent treatment of accountability in public schooling, see McGuinn, P. (2006). *No Child Left behind and the Transformation of Federal Education Policy, 1965–2005*. Lawrence, KS: University of Kansas Press. For an historical treatment going back further, see Kliebard, H. (1986). *The Struggle for the American Curriculum, 1893–1958*. New York: Routledge.

5. An archival film of a portion of Lyndon Johnson's speech at the University of Michigan, May 22, 1964, is available here: (www.c-span.org/video/?153610-1/great-society-speech).

6. Harrington, M. (1962). *The Other America: Poverty in the United States*. New York: Macmillan Publishers.

7. Conant, J. (1961). *Slums and Suburbs: A Commentary on Schools in Metropolitan Areas*. New York: McGraw-Hill.

8. Elementary and Secondary Education Act of 1965, Title II, sec. 201, Public Law 89–10, April 11, 1965, Government Printing Office, p. 27ff. Accessed 11/1/18: www.gpo.gov/fdsys/pkg/STATUTE-79/pdf/STATUTE-79-Pg27.pdf

9. Elementary and Secondary Education Act of 1965, Title II, section 205 a (5).

10. Darling-Hammond, L. (2010). *The Flat World and Education: How America's Commitment to Equity Will Determine Our Future*. New York: Teachers College Press.

11. For an analysis, see Darling-Hammond, *The Flat World and Education*, 18–23.

12. The Core Knowledge Foundation may be found at: www.coreknowledge.org

13. See Ravitch, D., & Finn, C. (1987). *What Do Our 17-Year-Olds Know? A Report on the First National Assessment of History and Literature*. New York: HarperCollins. In recent decades, Ravitch's view of testing has changed dramatically. See Ravitch, D. (2000). *The Death and Life of the Great American School System: How Testing and Choice Are Undermining Education*. New York: Basic Books.

14. NBC Olympics: Diving 101, Scoring. Accessed 5/10/19: http://archivepyc.nbcolympics.com/news/diving-101-scoring

15. See Opposs, D. (2016). Whatever happened to school-based assessment in England's GCSEs and A-levels? *Perspectives in Education, 34*(4), 52–61. doi:10.18820/2519593X/pie.v34i4.4

16. Combining several sources, we estimate that between 1999 and 2010, the Gates Foundation and the U.S. Department of Education invested over $3 billion in an effort to create small schools or convert large schools to small schools in the public sector.

> United States Department of Education, Smaller Learning Communities Program. Accessed 11/1/18: www2.ed.gov/programs/slcp/funding.html. This source shows the U.S. Department of Education invested $1,097,000,000 between 2000 and 2009.

> Gates, W. (2009). *2009 Annual Letter from Bill Gates*. Seattle, WA: Gates Foundation. Accessed 11/1/18: https://docs.gatesfoundation.org/Documents/2009-bill-gates-annual-letter.pdf. This source indicates "over $2 billion" (p. 11) invested by the Gates Foundation.

> See also Shaw, L. (2006, November 5). Foundation's small schools experiment has yet to yield big results. *Seattle Times*. Accessed 11/1/18: www.seattletimes.com/seattle-news/foundations-small-schools-experiment-has-yet-to-yield-big-results/

17. Lawrence Public Schools. (2017). *Welcome Back Letter to Parents Packet.* Accessed 11/1/18: www.lawrence.k12.ma.us/files/lps/LPSparentsguardians/Welcome_back_letter_to_parents_packet.pdf
18. See Au, W. (2009). *High Stakes Testing and the Standardization of Inequality.* New York: Routledge.
19. Mintrop, H., & Sunderman, G. L. (2009). *Why High Stakes Accountability Sounds Good But Doesn't Work: And Why We Keep on Doing It Anyway.* Los Angeles, CA: The Civil Rights Project and Proyecto Derechos Civiles at UCLA. Accessed 2/22/19: www.civilrightsproject.ucla.edu
20. Doyle, W. (1983). Academic work. *Review of Educational Research, 53*(2), 159–199. doi:10.2307/1170383
21. Opposs, Whatever happened to school-based assessment in England's GCSEs and A-levels?, 52–61.
22. Sommeiller, E., & Price, M. (2018). The new gilded age: Income inequality in the U.S. by state, metropolitan area, and county. *Economic Policy Institute.* Accessed 2/22/19: www.epi.org
23. Institute for Criminal Policy Research. (2016). *World Prison Brief: Highest to Lowest Prison Population Rate.* Author. Accessed 2/22/19: www.prisonstudies.org
24. Chetty, R., Grusky, D., Hell, M., Hendren, N., Manduca, R., & Narang, J. (2017, April 24). The fading American dream: Trends in absolute income mobility since 1940. *Science.* doi:10.1126/science.aal4617
25. Nicholas Donohue, President of the Nellie Mae Education Foundation, suggested the metaphor of the "unlocked cage" during a panel discussion at the Fall Forum of the Coalition of Essential Schools in 2016 (December 1–3, Providence, RI), attended by the author.
26. Chira, S. (1989, December 8). NYT governors and presidential aides hear advice on education goals. *The New York Times,* p. 34.
27. DeWitt, K. (1991, April 24). Vermont gauges learning by what's in portfolio. *The New York Times,* p. A23.
28. Koretz, D. (1992). *The Vermont Portfolio Assessment Program: Interim Report on Implementation and Impact, 1991–92 School Year.* Los Angeles, CA: National Center for Research on Evaluation, Standards, and Student Testing.
29. Koretz, D., Stecher, B., Klein, S., & McCaffrey, F. (1995). *The Vermont Portfolio Assessment Program: Findings and Implications.* Santa Monica, CA: RAND Corporation. www.rand.org/pubs/reprints/RP366.html
30. For more about recent developments with performance-based assessment, we recommend the following:

> Guha, R., Wagner, T., Darling-Hammond, L., Taylor, T., & Curtis, D. (2018). *The Promise of Performance Assessments: Innovations in High School Learning and College Admission.* Palo Alto, CA: Learning Policy Institute.
>
> Marion, S. F., & Buckley, K. (2016). Design and implementation considerations of performance-based and authentic assessments for use in accountability systems. In H. Braun (Ed.), *Meeting the Challenges to Measurement in an Era of Accountability.* New York, NY: Routledge and Taylor & Francis.
>
> New Hampshire Department of Education. (2016). *Moving from Good to Great in New Hampshire: Performance Assessment of Competency Education (PACE).* Concord, NH: New Hampshire Department of Education.

Rothman, R., & Marion, S. F. (2016). The next generation of state assessment and accountability. *Kappan*, *97*(8), 34–37. This article provides an overview of the NH system, emphasizing that it is based on Elmore's idea of reciprocal accountability. Teachers are being trained to design and use high quality local assessments and working collaboratively across districts to do so.

31. The Massachusetts Consortium for Innovative Education Assessment may be found at: www.mciea.org

8 Organization

In the era of No Child Left Behind, 'school turnaround' became a national industry. Driven by the political necessity to show results in the short term, consultants responded with strategies that reliably raised standardized test scores, sometimes dramatically, within one to two years. But such gains were typically achieved through focused test prep and alignment of instruction with tested content—an approach that was not new, but intensified under NCLB. Such strategies redirect existing practice without doing much to improve it. In 2010, the global management firm, McKinsey and Company, released a study by Mona Mourshed and others showing this approach widely in use, not just by turn-around consultants but by education systems internationally, using it as their theory of action for improvement.[1] We now know that top-down mandates and scripted curriculum reliably move schools from poor performance to minimally acceptable performance on national and international tests.

Proponents argue this is a necessary "first step" up the staircase to excellence; however, the same international research showing how schools move from poor to mediocre, also shows that moving schools from mediocre to excellent requires a nearly opposite set of policies and practices based on cooperation and a reflective work culture. That raises the question of whether command and control is a legitimate first step—or a dead end. The answer is intuitive. A cook trained at McDonald's may eventually become a fast food expert but is not on a path to cheffing at a restaurant known for fresh, nutritious, and creative cuisine. It is therefore no surprise that while such policies and practices improve test results in low-performing schools, they also reduce the capacity of high-performing schools to continue to offer a rich curriculum.[2] In short, persisting with this approach will tend to move everybody in the system toward the minimum. Intensifying such practices will foster widespread mediocrity. While the teaching norms in some schools are particularly troubling, we wonder if there are *different* first steps that can be taken. What if our national and global aspiration is something grander than the minimum for all? What if we imagine schools that regularly foster the kind of teaching and learning excellence described in this book? In that case we need a different theory of action.

In the early 1970s, a young researcher hired by the Rand Corporation began studying the implementation of four, federally-funded school innovation programs. The programs were based on a conventional change theory of the time: set clear goals, provide funding, provide training, and assume that implementation with fidelity will result. In short, policy at the top will dictate practice at the bottom. In several papers published between 1974 and 1978, the young researcher at Rand and her team concluded that policy does not, in fact, dictate practice, that local context matters, and that many players exercise agency in the shaping of classroom learning, through a process they termed "mutual adaptation." Milbrey McLaughlin is now an emeritus professor at Stanford University, and *The Rand Change Agent Study* has stood the test of time.[3]

McLaughlin's "mutual adaptation," it turns out, is a seminal principle for anyone who wants to understand how organizations operate. Human agency has a way of asserting itself all along the path of influence. That's because any organization is a collection of semi-autonomous individuals, each of whom can bump an innovation this way or that ensuring the final outcome is nearly unpredictable. Individuals matter. Individual actions matter. Democracy, it turns out, is not just a political ideology, it is a fundamental mechanism of human social organization, whether or not we endorse it. So how do we foster organizational change that acknowledges this fact? To answer that question, we turn first to a relatively new field of study, the goal of which is to understand what drives systems that are enormously complex, systems that defy conventional theories about organizations, change and leadership. Then we turn to an approach for school level and system level change, called organizational learning, that has developed from our understanding of complex systems. In the following chapter, we introduce six approaches to organizational learning. Each one has been thoughtfully refined over years of widespread use in schools. We conclude the book with a relevant teaching from Buddhist tradition.

Respecting Complexity

In the second half of the 20th century, scholars in the natural sciences, physics, and mathematics began to realize that simple cause-effect relationships failed to explain certain complex phenomena: weather and climate, ecosystems, ocean currents. For example, the American physicist, Philip Anderson, advanced a theory he called broken symmetry, which asserted that complex phenomena follow different rules. In a seminal paper published in

Science magazine in 1972, he wrote: "The behavior of large and complex elementary aggregates, it turns out, is not to be understood in terms of a simple extrapolation of the properties of a few particles. Instead at each level of complexity, entirely new properties appear."[4] Anderson and others were breaking new ground in the understanding of complexity. For his work, Anderson was awarded the Nobel prize in 1977.

During the 1970s, scholars in the social sciences began to consider parallel phenomena in the human social world: cities, governments, business organizations. Fields of study with exotic-sounding names emerged from many sources: systems theory, population ecology, complexity research, and, the most exotic of all, chaos theory. James Gleick's 1987 book popularized chaos theory, the study of enormously complex phenomena that surround us in daily life: the movement of water in a tub after you swish it with your hand, the path that smoke travels as it rises from a burning cigarette, the way cars move around an urban highway network, the formation of clouds.[5] These phenomena could not be understood by the deterministic practices of scientists seeking to isolate variables. There were simply way too many variables to comprehend. And maybe the very idea of variables, i.e., discrete entities with properties of their own, did not apply. Likewise, the usual rules governing change (big variable produces big change, little variable produces little change) did not apply. Gleick summarily dispatched such rules with his description of the now-famous "butterfly effect," this being "the notion that a butterfly stirring the air today in Peking can transform storm systems next month in New York."[6] Change in vast systems was not necessarily driven by large distinct forces. At the heart of this new field of study, as it relates to human social organization, was the "complex adaptive system."[7] To understand this term, we will break it down and then explain its relevance to the work of transformation within education.

Complex

Consider the toilet. The flush and refill mechanism of a conventional toilet is simple. The flush mechanism is triggered, which lifts the drain stopper at the bottom of the toilet tank. Water rushes out of the tank. Once the water is out, the drain stopper falls back into place and the tank begins to fill. As the tank fills, a floating valve rises. When the valve reaches the full line, it closes the tank's faucet and the system remains idle until the next flush. Simple. Complexity theory calls the action of the toilet flush a feedback loop—actions that respond sequentially from a trigger. The feedback loop for a toilet is simple.

Now consider a driverless car. Sensors all around the car read road conditions. Input from the sensors feed into a computer programmed to respond uniquely to hundreds of inputs in different combinations, changing by the second. A large obstruction ahead may ready the brakes for deployment. If the obstruction moves out of the way, the gas pedal may get primed. If the obstruction remains, the steering wheel may be primed for avoidance or the seat belts and airbags may be primed to engage if a crash appears unavoidable. And so on.[8] This is a complex system. The feedback loops are not simple sequences but complex algorithms, responding to multiple, ongoing inputs that govern brake, gas, steering, lights, horn, seatbelts, airbags, etc.

Adaptive

While the driverless car is more complex than a toilet, both are predictable systems. One is governed by mechanical parts and simple physics, the other is governed by algorithms. One is more complicated than the other, but, ultimately, both are predictable. That's because neither the toilet nor the driverless car exercises agency. Both require a human, ultimately, to direct its activity. The actions of both the toilet and the driverless car are predictable because their range of responses has been designed by humans. But what if the system is made up of humans? What if the components of a complex system are themselves complex systems? People are, themselves complex systems, so complex, in fact, that they exercise something called agency. Without descending into a debate of free will vs. determinism, or a digression into the fascinating field of artificial intelligence, we are going to assume a stance about human agency that is moderate, widely supported by contemporary psychology, and common sense. It is this: humans both *influence* and *are influenced by* their environment.[9] The essence of agency is the ability to learn from experience, and invent and execute new responses. Such behavior is termed *adaptive*. Adaptive systems defy prediction because they learn. Indeed, they are made of many individual agents, each of whom learns. When all the elements of a system possess this adaptive ability, complexity goes through the roof. Consider a classroom with 29 students and one teacher. Each student possesses personal traits that incline him or her to respond in various ways. Each student is part way through a day that has already included thousands of small and large experiences—visceral, emotional, and cognitive. Meanwhile, each student has a history of prior interaction with the other students in the class in a wide range of combinations. Then there's the teacher. Same thing, only the teacher has a plan which is coupled with a set of beliefs about her own efficacy and her students' efficacy. Given all these conditions, just about anything can happen when they all arrive in the same room at 1:17pm, after lunch, for something called social studies, and, just after students settle in their seats and the class quiets for the teacher, a kid in the front row farts audibly. Think butterfly effect. It should not surprise us that, as the old aphorism states: *The great mystery in any classroom is what anybody is learning.*[10]

System

A system is a bounded entity made up of components that interact. In the world of molecules, a sub-atomic particle is not a system, but a combination of atoms forming molecules and interacting with other atoms and molecules is a system. In the world of people, a person is not a system (though, in the world of cells, a person is an enormous system), but two or more people engaged together in some way are a system. Systems interact with other systems, some adjacent and overlapping, sometimes nested. This leads us to the point that is relevant to school change, namely that *schools are complex adaptive systems* which interact with adjacent and overlapping systems, and are nested among large and smaller systems.

How does this relate to educational change? If you want to change the amount of water in a single flush of the toilet, you adjust the float. It's simple. If you want to deepen the learning experience of the majority of students in a school, you . . . well . . . not so simple. The point is this: rules governing change in relatively simple, mechanistic systems do not apply to complex adaptive systems. We need different rules.

In 1997, Kevin Dooley, an engineering professor at the University of Minnesota, published a review of business management scholarship that in recent decades was moving complexity theory from the physical world to the world of human organizations.[11] Applying complexity theory to organizational change, Dooley concluded:

> The only true statement that could be made about the nature of change in a CAS is that there is not necessarily a consistent pattern of change. Change may occur rapidly or slowly; it may accumulate linearly or non-linearly; it may be constant or have bursts of punctuated equilibrium; it may be resisted or encouraged; it may take little or many resources; it may have a profound or no effect on system outcomes (p. 89).

For anyone interested in advancing organizational change, this is a shocking conclusion, raising the question, *Does complexity theory provide any insight beyond the disheartening implication that nothing can be done?* In fact, it does.

Complexity research, as reported by Dooley in the same article, has found that institutions with a strong organizational identity tend to produce within individuals a powerful framework for understanding the surrounding environment. Therefore, paraphrasing the article, the potentially efficacious first steps for an organizational leader are to develop a shared vision and build teams. A second step is to increase the flow of information to individual members and encourage analysis and reflection in order to inform action with a perspective grounded in the organization's broader reality. Dooley suggested some general guidelines:

> (a) create a shared purpose, (b) cultivate inquiry, learning, experimentation, and divergent thinking, (c) enhance external and internal interconnections via communication and technology, (d) instill rapid feedback loops for self-reference and self-control, (e) cultivate diversity, specialization, differentiation, and integration, (f) create shared values and principles of action, and (g) make explicit a few but essential structural and behavioral boundaries (pp. 92–93).

This strategy is precisely what was found in Mona Mourshed's study. In the simplest terms, the most effective approach appears to be that top-level management provides vision and support for capacity building while classroom-level practitioners, guided by the vision, engage in inquiry-oriented collaboration (capacity building) supported by top management. Thus, state-of-the-art educational improvement theory posits a marriage of top-down and bottom-up energies for high performance. The top provides a system-wide vision for improvement, accountability, and support for capacity building; the bottom exercises limited autonomy (bounded by the system vision) while engaging in intelligent, collaborative action, action that relies on both internal knowledge and external resources to build capacity.[12] Where does this leave us with respect to schools and classrooms? Before moving to the practical application of these ideas for system change, we need to follow one more historical tributary that explains how schools operate.

Organizational Learning

We know that individuals learn and grow, and we know that, with guidance, learning and growth can be enhanced. That's why we have schools. But what we did not know, until recent decades, is that organizations can learn and grow, too.

In the 1930s, a German-American psychologist, Kurt Lewin, began to question the traditional academic view that *applied* research was less important than and merely derivative of *basic* research. Sensing that context matters to the understanding of forces which shape a social situation, Lewin developed a kind of research that involved data gathering and analysis of a social situation by its principal players for the purpose of solving a problem specific to that context. He called this action research. Lewin's thinking spread through his writing and work he conducted at the Research Center for Group Dynamics at MIT, and the further work of his students. Over time, it spread to organizations as a means to improve outcomes. By the 1950s, a new field, 'organizational development (OD),' emerged.[13] It didn't take long for OD practitioners to realize that distinct organizational interventions could become an iterative process and that the learning obtained would be an ongoing project by and for the organization in which it was embedded. An organization could learn, and learning could become a deliberate, ongoing enterprise.

Crucial to the development of organizational learning were the twin notions of "single" and "double-loop" learning pioneered by Chris Argyris. Argyris found that most work is carried on without questioning the assumptions that frame it, and that, often, the problems and inefficiencies associated with work come from those very assumptions. By stepping back, identifying the governing assumptions of an organization, and adjusting them, a much deeper level of learning occurred and transformative change resulted. Argyris called this "double loop" learning in contrast to the merely surface tinkering with unexamined processes which he called "single-loop" learning.[14] By the 1980s, organizational learning had emerged as a new field. It wasn't long before the principles and practices of organizational learning migrated to schools through the work of Kenneth Leithwood, Shirley Hord, Peter Senge, and others.[15] But it wasn't until the publication of Richard Dufour's *Professional Learning Communities at Work* in 1998, that organizational learning practices, sometimes already in schools under a different label or no label at all, had a unifying name. [16] Like other powerful constructs, however, the term travels better than the practices it stands for. PLC, in many places, is merely a new name for the same bad meetings.

Many Paths Forward

Recent decades have seen a flowering of organizational learning principles in schools. A dynamic relationship between leading practitioners and engaged scholars has led to the development of numerous practical strategies. We argue, as the final major tenet of this book, that OL principles and the wealth of field-tested strategies associated with them constitute the powerful means by which we will achieve the transformation of teaching and learning which we have advocated in this book. The power of these approaches emanates from their understanding of schools as complex adaptive systems, and the recognition that the agency of the principal actors is, and always has been, a crucial driver of change. We begin by clarifying the traits that mark a school as a learning organization. We then walk through several well-developed approaches.

Any educational organization with a learning orientation will evidence certain traits. These will be readily apparent to a visitor as routines and habits of individuals and groups:

- A continuous drive for adaptation/improvement of the core enterprise of the school, which is teaching and learning
- Inquiry, reflection, collaboration
- Evidence-based examination of teaching practice and student learning
- Shared responsibility for the school as a whole.
- A shared vision, mission, and values.

These traits will be apparent in the prominent features of school life. Table 8.1 offers a side-by-side comparison of schools with a conventional orientation; and schools with a learning orientation.

With these distinctions in mind, we turn to six organizational learning approaches developed specifically for schools. We offer these not as a prescription to be followed precisely, or as a menu of options. Rather, in the spirit

Table 8.1 Conventional School Practice; and School-as-Learning-Organization[17]

Conventional School Practice	School-as-Learning Organization
Leaders focus first and foremost on buildings, schedules, personnel, budget, program delivery.	Leaders focus first and foremost on teaching and learning, which drives decisions about schedules, budget, etc.
Existing patterns of privilege and marginalization go unexamined. The school reproduces inequality.	Leaders and teachers, committed to addressing historic inequities, challenge related behavior and seek practices that foster equity and learn from pluralism.
Teaching is based on externally developed programs, often scripted.	Teaching is adaptive, a blend of externally developed ideas and local innovations
Professional development is one-shot workshops to fix problems or entertain; little follow-up or accountability for change.	Professional learning is continuous, built into the work schedule, evidence-based; significant follow-through and accountability for growth.
Teaching practice is private. "Closed doors." Little to no critical discussion of instruction.	Teaching practice is shared. "Open doors," supportive, critical examination of practice with colleagues.
Guiding ethic: Quick solutions, immediate results.	Guiding ethic: Inquiry, evidence-based, continuous adaptation/improvement, long term growth.
School is a mini-bureaucracy: each person does his or her job.	School is a community: shared vision, shared responsibility for all students.

of adaptation, we expect that thoughtful readers will draw from these ideas and practices whatever makes sense for their own setting. Good work is almost always a blend of ideas picked up elsewhere with homemade innovation.

A Learning Community Begins With Shared Vision and Mission

Richard DuFour was a career educator who pioneered many of the practices now associated with professional learning communities during his tenure as a principal and superintendent in Illinois. In his "retirement," he became one of the most well-known experts on PLCs. Ads for his professional development company, Solution Tree, were a staple in such publications as *Education Week* and *Educational Leadership*. His book, *Professional Learning Communities at Work: Best Practices for Enhancing Student Achievement* first published in 1998, has been enormously influential in defining PLCs in school practice across the United States and elsewhere.[18] In fact, its success as a commercial product became a problem. Dufour lamented at the height of his influence, "the term has been used so ubiquitously that it is in danger of losing all meaning."[19] It appears that, like many school reform ideas, the language of the PLC spread quickly while practice has been much harder to root. Nonetheless, the original ideas developed by Dufour and colleagues, as opposed to the PLC label slapped on to the same old bad meetings, are a potent catalyst for teaching and learning.

Dufour argues that the work begins with a school community asking earnestly, "Why do we exist?" The answer to that question is a school's mission statement. Most schools have one and most school mission statements revolve around the idea that *all students can learn*. This, says Dufour, is where a crucial next step must be taken, a next step often neglected—which is why so many mission statements are meaningless. Dufour says a school must ask two vital questions: "1. If we believe all kids can learn, exactly what is it that we will expect them to learn? 2. If we believe all kids can learn, how do we respond when they do not learn?" (p. 59). The outworking of these questions necessarily leads to the development of a vision statement—"What do we hope to become?" and a statement of values— "How must we behave in order to make our shared vision a reality?" Only after a school is clear about its mission, vision, and values, can teachers engage in meaningful collaboration around the day to day work of student learning. And collaboration, Dufour argues, is crucial to "enable teachers to test ideas . . ., foster better decisions . . ., reduce fear of risk taking . . . and reinforce commitment to change initiatives" (p. 117). In Dufour's view, collaborative teams are the vehicle that drives organizational learning in a school. His company, Solution Tree, has developed a wealth of strategies for teams to use in continuously adapting and improving practice to enhance student learning.[20]

Collaboration is a crucial ingredient for any organizational learning scheme, and yet it remains in many places poorly understood. While school leaders will quickly agree that good schools require collaboration, put them in a room, tell them to start collaborating, and one of two things will likely result: chaos or silence. And the latter rarely happens with school administrators. Which is why the next approach we discuss is so helpful.

Collaboration Means Thinking Together

Central to organizational learning is collaboration. But collaboration is a kind of black box, as mysterious as it is widely invoked. What does it actually mean? What does it look like when people are doing it? At its best, collaboration is a generative process in which people *think together*. This may seem obvious, but, in fact, it is, for most of us, a foreign practice. Watch the dynamics of most workplace meetings and you will see that individuals tend to share opinions that were formed before the meeting began without really considering all the other opinions being lobbed around the room. The discussion is a battle to see whose idea will win. According to William Isaacs, co-founder with Peter Senge of MIT's Center for Organizational Learning, in most discussions, "people do not listen, they re-load."[21] What if we *did* listen? What if the discussion was the collective pursuit of a compelling question in which people *think together*, in the moment. And what if some simple rules were agreed upon by the group to ward off the problems of conventional discourse that block collaboration.

In the early 1990s, a group of educators working for the Coalition of Essential Schools began to experiment with rules for meetings that deliberately constrained discourse to avoid conversational pitfalls and make the discussion more generative. They used the word, "protocol," to describe this idea, and it stuck.[22] Fast forward 25 years, and "protocol" is widely recognized in education circles as a technique for running meetings. Rightly understood, a protocol is a powerful tool that can unlock the collective wisdom of the group. Unfortunately, however, like "PLC," protocols have been attempted in settings where the participants and/or facilitator engage in the work without understanding it. The results are predictably disastrous. So let's get it right. What follows is a short primer.

While the term, protocol, has different meanings in different contexts, in the context of education in recent decades the term has been adopted to describe a learning-focused conversation governed by formal, agreed-upon guidelines. Guidelines typically involve steps for the group to follow, rules about who can speak when and what questions may be addressed. They also compel careful listening. For example, the Success Analysis Protocol is designed to help a small group of educator colleagues learn from teaching successes they have experienced and apply the learning to their ongoing practice. The steps of the Success Analysis Protocol assist the group in sharing, clarifying, analyzing, and learning from each other's success. Here it is:

SUCCESS ANALYSIS PROTOCOL

Developed by Daniel Baron
Adapted from www.nsrfharmony.org by J. Nehring

Introduction

The purpose of this exercise is to identify effective elements of teaching, based on successes that members of the group have experienced in their own work. This exercise involves three colleagues, each of whom shares a teaching success that he or she has experienced. The group analyzes the success to understand what made it successful. After all three members have shared, the group as a whole looks for patterns across all three successes to identify practical insights for their ongoing work. The group may choose in advance to focus on an aspect of teaching, such as, critical thinking skills or questioning strategies.

This exercise is timed to ensure that all members may participate equally and to ensure that efficient use is made of a limited amount of time. People who use this exercise have found that it works best if you follow the steps and the time limits. If you follow the exercise as written, it will take just over a half-hour to complete.

The Protocol

Step 1: All members of the group think quietly to identify a teaching success that they have experienced. Each member should be prepared to describe what happened and what made it a success.
Take up to three minutes for this step.
Step 2: Decide who in the group will be presenter 1, 2, and 3. Note: when group member 1 is presenting, member 2 should keep time and facilitate. When member 2 is presenting, member 3 should keep time and facilitate. And so on.
Step 3: Presenter 1 presents his or her success, describing what happened and why it was particularly successful.
Take up to three minutes for this step.

Step 4: All three group members discuss the success, beginning with questions to clarify understanding and then moving into a discussion of the success.

> Sample clarifying questions:
>
> > Can you repeat what you said about X please?
> > I wasn't sure what you meant when you said X. Can you clarify that please?
>
> Sample discussion comments:
>
> > This is what I heard . . .
> > This is what stands out . . .
> > What strikes me about why this was successful is . . .
> > This is different from the norm because . . .
> > Something I didn't hear that surprised me was . . .

Take seven minutes for this step.

Step 5: Repeat Steps 3 and 4 for each group member. When repeating Steps 3 and 4, refrain from comparing presenters' successes. This comes later. If you think of an interesting connection to another presenter's success, make a note of it.

Step 6: As a group, consider all three successes and ask yourselves:

> 1. What patterns do we see among these successes? Make a list
> 2. What practical insights may we apply to our teaching practice? Make a list.

Take ten minutes for this step.

You might ask, why use a protocol? Why not just have a regular-old discussion about teaching and learning? The answer is 'regular-old' discussions often go off the rails. Regular-old discussions frequently wander from the topic, or leave vital participants unengaged, or become mired in unspoken interpersonal tensions—patterns that alienate rather than enlighten. This is bad enough for casual conversation, but in a workplace, it stifles creativity, demoralizes co-workers, and blocks progress. A well-facilitated protocol remedies these problems.

- A protocol ensures that the conversation stays focused on an agreed upon topic and an agreed upon purpose. We have all experienced the frustration of a professional discussion which wanders off topic and accomplishes nothing. Using the protocol helps avoid this problem.
- A protocol ensures that the job gets done in a given amount of time. Educators are busy people who need to use their time productively. A

protocol lets all the participants know in advance how much time will be needed and then provides time indicators for each step to ensure that the entire protocol is completed in the time allotted for it.

- A protocol ensures that all voices are heard. We have all experienced the frustration of a professional discussion in which a small minority of the participants speak up, robbing the group of the benefit of everyone's thinking. The steps of a protocol help ensure that all voices are heard and learning is amplified and deepened by the insights of each member and the collective wisdom of the group.
- A protocol creates an emotionally safe environment that promotes deep learning. Most protocols involve participants sharing aspects of their own practice. Doing so involves some risk. There may be criticism. The steps of the protocol help to ensure that opening up one's practice to the group is done in a thoughtful, constructive, and emotionally safe environment.
- A protocol helps to mine the wisdom of the group and create new knowledge, constructed from the group's collective thinking. This is, potentially, the most powerful aspect of a protocol.

The Success Analysis Protocol, above, is not particularly risky. People like talking about success and the protocol builds in affirmation. But what if we want to learn from a workplace *problem*? What if we want to enter into that zone where I, as an educator, am unsure what to do about something I fear I do not fully understand? Typically, we hide these kinds of problems for fear of exposing ourselves as incompetent. What's true, however, is we all experience problems like this from time to time and they are the sort of problem that would especially benefit from careful analysis by a group of smart colleagues who trust each other enough to give honest input. There are numerous protocols designed specifically for these more difficult conversations, and the emotional safety that the protocol provides opens a path to powerful solutions.

One final thought before we leave our discussion of protocols. Protocols can feel pretty weird. They violate the unwritten rules of 'normal' conversation, but they do so for important reasons. If you are new to protocols, it is important to acknowledge just how foreign they feel, but go with the weirdness and just see, when you come out the other side, if it was worth it. We think you'll agree that it was.

Protocols are very useful tools for professional learning. At the same time, a protocol is only a tool. It has uses and it has limitations. It is important for us to remember that the protocol is not the purpose. Learning is the purpose. Also, while protocols are usually used by adults in a professional learning context, they can be used or adapted for use by students in classroom settings. Various protocols have been invented to serve different purposes. There are several excellent sources for learning about protocols. They include a book, *The Power of Protocols*,[23] and several websites.[24]

Evidence Over Opinions

Schools are drowning in data. Mostly from test results, but also from surveys, demographic reports, attendance records, and the like. In many schools, the data provides no more than a summary judgment, often harsh, that signals success or failure—think the annual rollout of test scores. Some schools, however, use data to inform, revise, and enhance teaching and learning. That's where *DataWise* comes in.

DataWise began as a collaboration by a small group of Boston school leaders, doctoral students at Harvard's Graduate School of Education, and Harvard faculty (notably Richard Murnane—see Chapter One). They wondered how the reams of existing data in schools might be put to work for school improvement, and they began to experiment. Within several years, they had evolved a system. On the surface, the system entails a step-wise process, but DataWise leaders recognized in their early work with schools that for the process to succeed, a distinct culture must be in place.

The DataWise process is an eight-step cycle

1) Organize for collaborative work
2) Build assessment literacy
3) Create data overview
4) Dig into student data
5) Examine instruction
6) Develop action plan
7) Plan to assess progress
8) Act and assess[25]

The eight steps can be understood broadly as three phases: preparing, inquiring, and acting.

This model has proven powerfully efficacious in schools that follow it with fidelity. However, the work will not move forward without the culture to support it. The DataWise people call this culture the ACE Habits of Mind:

- A shared commitment to action, assessment, and adjustment
- Intentional collaboration
- A relentless focus on evidence[26]

Not surprisingly, collaboration in the DataWise process is organized using protocols, like those discussed above. But what DataWise brings most notably to the work of school transformation is the marriage of collaboration and evidence. School folks are accustomed to sharing opinions, a habit readily apparent in most school meetings. But we are less practiced in pausing to observe, simply *to see*, and then to build our thinking from the *evidence*, as opposed to a pre-conception. The power of this simple yet very difficult shift of habit should not be underestimated. It is the difference between a community that is learning and a whole lot of jaw flapping.

Developing Instructional Practice

There is a powerful unwritten rule in most schools that says, 'I won't judge your teaching, and don't you dare judge mine.' It comes from a profound insecurity about what constitutes good teaching, and the conflict that ensues when any judgment about teaching is rendered. It comes also from a long tradition in teaching of privacy and autonomy.[27] In most schools, there is little agreement about practice, neither the language to talk about it nor the essence of what makes it 'good.' But we know that a school will not flourish without a shared vision for instruction. How do we break through?

The idea behind 'instructional rounds,' also developed at Harvard University, is that educators observe classrooms in teams much like physicians doing medical rounds.[28] Initial discussion is strictly observational. Like other approaches to organizational learning that we've discussed, instructional rounds relies on suspension of judgment and resisting the urge to move up the ladder of inference before gathering data. 'What did we see?' is the question that guides early conversation. The rounds process begins with a problem rooted in teaching practice that the school is working on. For example, a high school may be trying to increase the instructional demand for higher level cognitive skills in all classrooms. Teams then will observe classrooms with an eye to the problem. Discussion, at first, focuses strictly on what was observed. Then it moves to analysis and diagnosis. Changes are recommended, implemented, and assessed. Because the work is done by a team, shared language and a shared vision of practice builds as the team works together and becomes a learning community.[29]

Deepening Instructional Practice

Like instructional rounds, another approach called 'lesson study' focuses intently on what happens in classrooms. Whereas an instructional rounds team typically include individuals other than the teachers being observed, lesson study involves primarily those teachers whose practice is the focus of the work. At the center is a lesson—often co-designed by a group of teachers who then closely observe the lesson as it is taught by one member of the team. Observers pay particularly close attention to the students, and how are *they* experiencing this lesson. The team then discusses the lesson focusing on evidence of learning, as opposed to judgment about the teacher. The team revises the lesson and members re-teach it, often with observers present, and the process continues. Lesson study originated in Japan, where it is regularly and widely practiced.[30]

Many Paths, One Goal

There are many ways to cultivate a learning community. The most powerful approach will be the one that a team of educators chooses for itself in response to the opportunities and constraints of their local context. At the heart of the work is a fierce commitment to the ongoing improvement of teaching and learning achieved through inquiry, reflection, collaboration, observation, and the close scrutiny of evidence.[31] In this chapter, we have provided a brief introduction to several well developed, widely used systems for organizational learning. We encourage educators to explore each one further, using the references we have provided, in order to craft an approach that makes sense in their school.

In the studies we conducted, teachers doing exemplary work in the schools we visited operated largely without the support of well-developed learning organizations. Perhaps that is why they were in the minority. It should not come as a surprise that teachers featured in the AIR study examined in Chapter Four of this book, worked in schools with a strong commitment to collaborative inquiry nested in networks of schools that learned regularly from each other. The result was whole schools in which exemplary practice was the norm.

Notes

1. Mourshed, M., Chijioke, C., & Barber, M. (2010). *How the World's Most Improved School Systems Keep Getting Better.* London: McKinsey & Company.
2. Wilder, T., Jacobsen, R., & Rothstein, R. (2008). *Grading Education: Getting Accountability Right.* New York: Teachers College Press, Economic Policy Institute and Wiley.
3. Berman, P., & McLaughlin, M. (1974). *Federal Programs Supporting Educational Change, Vol. I: A Model of Educational Change.* Santa Monica, CA: RAND Corporation. This is the first of five volumes, all of which are available at: www.rand.org/pubs/reports/R1589z1.html. See also McLaughlin, M. (1990). The Rand change agent study revisited: Macro perspectives and micro realities. *Educational Researcher, 19*(9), 11–16. This paper revisits the original study, largely affirming its main findings and suggesting modifications.
4. Anderson, P. W. (1972). More is different. *Science, 177*(4047), 393–396. doi:10.1126/science.177.4047.393

5. Gleick, J. (1987). *Chaos: The Making of a New Science*. New York: Viking. See p. 9 and ff.
6. The origin of the phrase, "butterfly effect," is Lorenz, E. N. (1963). Deterministic nonperiodic flow. *Journal of the Atmospheric Sciences*, *20*(2), 130–141. doi:10.1175/1520-0469(1963)020<0130:dnf>2.0.co;2
7. See, for example, Miller, J., & Page, S. (2007). *Complex Adaptive Systems: An Introduction to Computational Models of Social Life*. Princeton, NJ: Princeton University Press. Also, Holland, J. (2014). *Complexity: A Very Short Introduction*. Oxford, UK: Oxford University Press.
8. For information about driverless cars, go to https://auto.howstuffworks.com/under-the-hood/trends-innovations/driverless-car2.htm
9. Albert Bandura has advanced the model of "reciprocal causation." Bandura, A. (1989). Human agency in social cognitive theory. *American Psychologist*, *44*(9), 1175–1184. ". . . people partly determine the nature of their environment and are influenced by it." (p. 1182).
10. We are unable to locate a source for this statement. We heard it first many years ago from William Wojcik, a wise English teacher at Bethlehem Central High School, Delmar, NY.
11. Dooley, K. (1997). A complex adaptive systems model of organization change. *Non-Linear Dynamics, Psychology, and Life Sciences*, *1*(1), 67–97.
12. For a fuller treatment of these ideas, see Nehring, J., & O'Brien, E. (2012). Strong agents and weak systems: University support for school level improvement. *Journal of Educational Change*, *13*(4), 449–485. doi:10.1007/s10833-012-9187-0
13. For a summary, see Scott, B. (2009). *Organization Development Primer: Change Management, Kurt Lewin and Beyond*. Belfast, Northern Ireland: Queens University.
14. Argyris, C., & Schön, D. (1978). *Organizational Learning: A Theory of Action Perspective*. Reading, MA: Addison Wesley.
15. See the following:

> Hord, S. (1997). *Professional Learning Communities: Communities of Continuous Learning and Improvement*. Austin, TX: Southwest Educational Development Lab.
>
> Leithwood, K., & Louis, K. (Eds.). (1998). *Organizational Learning in Schools*. Abingdon, UK: Taylor & Francis.
>
> Senge, P., Cambron-McCabe, N., Lucas, T., Smith, B., & Dutton, J. (2000). *Schools That Learn: A Fifth Discipline Fieldbook for Educators, Parents, and Everyone Who Cares about Education*. New York: Doubleday.

16. Dufour, R., & Eaker, R. (1998). *Professional Learning Communities at Work: Best Practices for Enhancing Student Achievement*. Bloomington, IN: National Educational Service.
17. For a fuller presentation of relevant research, see Nehring, J., & O'Brien, E. (2012). Strong agents and weak systems: University support for school level improvement. *Journal of Educational Change*, *13*(4), 449–485.
18. Dufour & Eaker, *Professional Learning Communities at Work*.
19. Dufour, R. (2004). What is a professional learning community? *Educational Leadership*, *61*(8), 6–11.
20. Solution Tree. Accessed 5/10/19 at www.solutiontree.com.
21. Isaacs, W. (1999). *Dialogue: The Art of Thinking Together*. New York: Doubleday, 18.

22. See McDonald, J., Mohr, N., Dichter, A., & McDonald, E. (2007). *The Power of Protocols: An Educator's Guide to Better Practice*. New York: Teachers College Press. See, especially, p. xi and following.

23. McDonald, et al., *The Power of Protocols*.

24. Go to any of the following websites: www.schoolreforminitiative.org; www.nsrfharmony.org; www.rightquestion.org

25. Boudett, K., City, E., & Murnane, R. (2013). *Data Wise: A Step-by-Step Guide to Using Assessment Results to Improve Teaching and Learning*. Cambridge, MA: Harvard Education Press. Also https://datawise.gse.harvard.edu

26. Boudett, et al., *Data Wise*, 31ff.

27. Lortie, D. (1975). *School Teacher: A Sociological Study*. Chicago: University of Chicago Press.

28. What is now widely known as Instructional Rounds began, as far as we could determine, in 1995, when Steve Seidel at Harvard University's Project Zero began convening area educators for discussions of teaching practice. The "medical rounds" metaphor was explicit in their early work. Later, doctoral students and faculty in the Harvard Graduate School of Education picked up the idea and developed it into a formal network process. Also, the Clark University Education Department, under Thomas Del Prete, pioneered rounds in the late 1990s. To learn more about the backstory, go to: www.gse.harvard.edu/news/ed/09/09/round-round

29. City, E., Elmore, R., Fiarman, S., & Teitel, L. (2009). *Instructional Rounds in Education: A Network Approach to Improving Teaching and Learning*. Cambridge, MA: Harvard Education Press.

30. An excellent resource to learn more about lesson study is Stepanek, J., Appel, G., Leong, M., Mangan, M., & Mitchell, M. (2007). *Leading Lesson Study: A Practical Guide for Teachers and Facilitators*. Thousand Oaks, CA: Corwin Press.

31. Dana, N., & Yendol-Hoppey, D. (2008). *The Reflective Educator's Guide to Professional Development: Coaching Inquiry-Oriented Learning Communities*. Thousand Oaks, CA: Corwin Press. This book describes a straightforward approach to collaborative inquiry rooted in the early work of scholars who developed action research, on which all of the approaches described in this chapter were developed.

Final Thoughts: Excellence Is a Discipline

Buddhist monk Thich Nhat Hanh has famously pointed out that one cannot achieve peace through war. If the end is peace, then the means, too, must be peaceful. "There is no path to peace; the path is peace."[1] Likewise, we won't achieve inspired learning in our students through organizational approaches that squash agency and intelligence. The traits to which we aspire must be the discipline the we, at all levels of the system, practice from the start. There is no path to excellent schools. The path is excellence.

Excellence, however, has never been such a narrow idea as it is in schools today. In the space of a few decades, public accountability metrics have reshaped our public schools, in open defiance of educators, academics, and policy leaders. What now meets the standard of 'high performance' is a thin gruel of uninspired teaching to disengaged students. Such practices have intensified social inequalities. In this book, we have made the case for a re-definition of excellence in teaching and learning that is rooted in academic research, the broad consensus of policy thought-leaders, the wisdom of teaching practice going back centuries, and pedagogy that seeks enrichment from our cultural pluralism. We also describe the school and system level supports needed to foster schools and classrooms that are intellectually alive for all students. At a time when a system run amok asks obsessively, 'how do we measure X?' we need to re-center our focus by asking instead, 'How do we inspire and engage *all* our children and youth?'

Note

1. This quote is widely attributed to Thich Nhat Hanh, but the source could not be verified.

Bibliography

Adams, C. F. (1879). The new departure in the common schools of Quincy. In S. Cohen (Ed.), *Education in the United States: A Documentary History* (pp. 33–40). New York: Random House, 1974, 3, 1811.

Aikin, W. (1942). *The Story of the Eight-Year Study*. New York: Harper & Row.

Allport, G. W. (1954). *The Nature of Prejudice*. Reading, MA: Addison Wesley.

American Diploma Project. (2004). *Ready or Not: Creating a High School Diploma That Counts*. Washington, DC: Achieve, Inc.

Anandiadou, K., & Claro, M. (2009). *21st Century Skills and Competences for New Millennium Learners in OECD Countries*. OECD Education Working Papers, No. 41. OECD Publishing.

Anderson, P. W. (1972). More is different. *Science, 177*(4047), 393–396. doi:10.1126/science.177.4047.393

Anyon, J. (1980). Social class and the hidden curriculum of work. *Journal of Education, 162*(1), 67–92, 83.

Apple, M. (1977). What do schools teach? *Curriculum Inquiry, 6*, 341–358.

Argyris, C., & Schön, D. (1978). *Organizational Learning: A Theory of Action Perspective*. Reading, MA: Addison Wesley.

Au, W. (2009). *High Stakes Testing and the Standardization of Inequality*. New York: Routledge.

Bandura, A. (1989). Human agency in social cognitive theory. *American Psychologist, 44*(9), 1175–1184.

Banks, J. A. (1971). Teaching Black history with a focus on decision making. *Social Education, 35*(7), 740–745, 820–821.

Banks, J. A., & McGee, C. (2015). *Multicultural Education: Issues and Perspectives* (9th ed.). Hoboken, NJ: Wiley.

Berman, P., & McLaughlin, M. (1974). *Federal Programs Supporting Educational Change, Vol. 1: A Model of Educational Change*. Santa Monica, CA: RAND Corporation. Bibliography.

Boudett, K., City, E., & Murnane, R. (2013). *Data Wise: A Step-by-Step Guide to Using Assessment Results to Improve Teaching and Learning*. Cambridge, MA: Harvard Education Press. https://datawise.gse.harvard.edu

Bourdieu, P., & Passeron, J. (1977). *Reproduction in Education, Society, and Culture*. Thousand Oaks, CA: Sage Publications.

Bowles, S., & Gintis, H. (1976). *Schooling in Capitalist America: Education and the Contradictions of Economic Life*. New York: Basic Books.

Boyer, E. (1983). *High School: A Report on Secondary Education in America*. New York: Harper & Row.

Bransford, J., Brown, A., & Cocking, R. (Eds.). (1999). *How People Learn: Brain, Mind, Experience, and School*. Washington, DC: National Academies Press.

Bunnell, T. (2010). The International Baccalaureate and a framework for class consciousness: The potential outcomes of a "class-for-itself". *Discourse: Studies in the Cultural Politics of Education*, *31*(3), 351–362.

Campbell, J. (1965). *The Children's Crusader: Colonel Francis W. Parker*. New York: Teachers College Press.

Carr, L. G. (1997). *"Color-Blind" Racism*. Thousand Oaks, CA: Sage Publications.

Chetty, R., Grusky, D., Hell, M., Hendren, N., Manduca, R., & Narang, J. (2017, April). The fading American dream: Trends in absolute income mobility since 1940. *Science*, *24*. doi:10.1126/science.aal4617

Chira, S. (1989, December 8). NYT governors and presidential aides hear advice on education goals. *The New York Times*, p. 34.

Chow, B. (2010). The quest for deeper learning. *Education Week*, *30*(26), 22–24.

City, E., Elmore, R., Riarman, S., & Teitel, L. (2009). *Instructional Rounds in Education: A Network Approach to Improving Teaching and Learning* (p. 30). Cambridge, MA: Harvard Education Press.

Conant, J. (1961). *Slums and Suburbs: A Commentary on Schools in Metropolitan Areas*. New York: McGraw-Hill.

Conley, D. (2003). *Understanding University Success: A Report from Standards for Success*. Eugene, OR: Center for Educational Policy Research. Accessed 2/22/19: https://eric.ed.gov/?id=ED476300, No. ED476300.

Core Knowledge Foundation. www.coreknowledge.org

Cremin, L. (1964). *The Transformation of the School: American Progressivism, 1876–1957*. New York: Vintage.

Cross, D. I. (2009). Alignment, cohesion, and change: Examining mathematics teachers' belief structures and their influence on instructional practices. *Journal of Mathematics Teacher Education*, *12*, 325–346.

Cuban, L. (1983). What did teachers teach? 1890–1980. *Theory into Practice*, *22*(3), 159–165.

Cuban, L. (1993). *How Teachers Taught, Constancy and Change in American Classrooms*. New York: Teachers College Press.

Dana, N., & Yendol-Hoppey, D. (2008). *The Reflective Educator's Guide to Professional Development: Coaching Inquiry-Oriented Learning Communities*. Thousand Oaks, CA: Corwin Press.

Darling-Hammond, L. (2010). *The Flat World and Education: How America's Commitment to Equity Will Determine Our Future*. New York: Teachers College Press.

Dede, C. (2010). Comparing frameworks for 21st century skills. In J. Bellanca & R. Brandt (Eds.), *21st Century Skills: Rethinking How Students Learn* (pp. 51–75). Bloomington, IN: Solution Tree Press.

Delgado, R., & Stefancic, J. (2001). *Critical Race Theory: An Introduction*. New York: New York University Press.

DeWitt, K. (1991, April 24). Vermont Gauges learning by what's in portfolio. *The New York Times*, p. A23.

Dooley, K. (1997). A complex adaptive systems model of organization change. *Non-Linear Dynamics, Psychology, and Life Sciences*, *1*(1), 67–97.

Doyle, W. (1983). Academic work. *Review of Educational Research*, *53*(2), 159–199. doi:10.2307/1170383

Dufour, R. (2004). What is a professional learning community? *Educational Leadership*, *61*(8), 6–11.

Dufour, R., & Eaker, R. (1998). *Professional Learning Communities at Work: Best Practices for Enhancing Student Achievement*. Bloomington, IN: National Educational Service.

Dukakis, M. (1988, October 14). Science policy. *Science*, *242*(4876), 173–178. doi:10.1126/science.173-a

Edmondson, A., & Roloff, K. (2009). Overcoming barriers to collaboration: Psychological safety and learning in diverse teams. In E. Salas, G. Goodwin, & C. Burke (Eds.), *Team Effectiveness in Complex Organizations: Cross-Disciplinary Perspectives and Approaches* (pp. 183–203). Abingdon, UK: Routledge, 2008.

Elementary and Secondary Education Act of 1965, Title II, sec. 201, Public Law 89-10, April 11, 1965, Government Printing Office, p. 27ff. Accessed 11/1/18: www.gpo.gov/fdsys/pkg/STATUTE-79/pdf/STATUTE-79-Pg27.pdf

Entry: Wilhelm von Humboldt, Baron. (1998). *Encyclopedia of World Biography*, Gale. Biography in Context. Accessed 11/10/17: libraries.state.ma.us

Frank-Gemmill, G. (2013). The IB Diploma and UK university degree qualifications. *Journal of Research in International Education*, *12*(1), 49–65.

Frobel, F. (1908). *The Education of Man* (W. N. Hailmann, Trans., pp. 54–55). New York: D. Appleton and Company. Accessed 2/22/19: https://archive.org/stream/educationofman00fruoft#page/n3/mode/2up

Gates, W. (2009). *2009 Annual Letter from Bill Gates*. Seattle, WA: Gates Foundation. Accessed 11/1/18: https://docs.gatesfoundation.org/Documents/2009-bill-gates-annual-letter.pdf

Gleick, J. (1987). *Chaos: The Making of a New Science*. New York: Viking.

Gonzalez, N., Moll, L., & Amanti, C. (2005). *Funds of Knowledge: Theorizing Practices in Households and Classrooms*. Mahwah, NJ: Lawrence Erlbaum Associates.

Goodlad, J. (1984). *A Place Called School*. New York: McGraw-Hill.

Gordon, M., Vanderkamp, E., & Halic, O. (2015). International Baccalaureate programmes in Title I schools in the United States: Accessibility, participation and university enrollment. *IB Research*. www.ibo.org/globalassets/publications/ib-research

Grafton, A. (1981). Wilhelm von Humboldt. *The American Scholar*, *50*(3), 371–381.

Guha, R., Wagner, T., Darling-Hammond, L., Taylor, T., & Curtis, D. (2018). *The Promise of Performance Assessments: Innovations in High School Learning and College Admission*. Palo Alto, CA: Learning Policy Institute.

Harrington, M. (1962). *The Other America: Poverty in the United States*. New York: Macmillan Publishers.

Hattie, J. (2009). *Visible Learning: A Synthesis of over 800 Meta-Analyses Relating to Achievement*. New York: Routledge.

Hawley, W. D. (2007). Designing schools that use student diversity to enhance learning of all students. In E. Frankenberg & G. Orfield (Eds.), *Lessons in Integration: Realizing the Promise of Racial Diversity in American Schools* (pp. 31–56). Charlottesville: University of Virginia Press.

Henke, R., Chen, X., & Goldman, G. (1999). *What Happens in Classrooms? Instructional Practices in Elementary and Secondary Schools, 1994–95* (NCES 1999-348). Washington, DC: U.S. Department of Education.

Hinde, E. R. (2003). The tyranny of the test: Elementary teachers' conceptualizations of the effects of state standards and mandated tests on their practice. *Current Issues in Education, 6*(10).

Hirsch, E. D. (1987). *Cultural Literacy: What Every American Needs to Know*. Boston: Houghton Mifflin.

Hirsch, E. D. (2010). *The Making of Americans: Democracy and Our Schools*. New Haven: Yale University Press.

Holland, J. (2014). *Complexity: A Very Short Introduction*. Oxford, UK: Oxford University Press.

Hord, S. (1997). *Professional Learning Communities: Communities of Continuous Learning and Improvement*. Austin, TX: Southwest Educational Development Lab.

How Stuff Works. https://auto.howstuffworks.com/under-the-hood/trends-innovations/driverless-car2.htm

Huberman, M., Bitter, C., Anthony, J., & O'Day, J. (2014). The shape of deeper learning: Strategies, structures and cultures in deeper learning network high schools. *American Institutes for Research*. www.air.org and *The Research Alliance for New York City Schools*. www.steinhardt.nyu.edu/research_alliance. Accessed 8/19/17: www.air.org

Institute for Criminal Policy Research. (2016). *World Prison Brief: Highest to Lowest Prison Population Rate*. Author. Accessed 2/22/19: www.prisonstudies.org

International Baccalaureate. www.ibo.org/programmes/find-an-ib-school/

International School of Geneva. www.ecolint.ch/overview/our-history

Isaacs, W. (1999). *Dialogue: The Art of Thinking Together*. New York: Doubleday.

Kahn, W. A. (1990). Psychological conditions of personal engagement and disengagement at work. *Academy of Management Journal, 33*(4), 692–724. doi:10.2307/25628

Katz, M. (1987). *Reconstructing American Education*. Cambridge, MA: Harvard University Press.

Kirschner, P., Sweller, J., & Clark, R. (2006). Why minimal guidance during instruction does not work: An analysis of the failure of constructivist, discovery, problem-based, experiential, and inquiry-based teaching. *Educational Psychologist, 41*(2), 75–86.

Klem, A. M., & Connell, J. P. (2004). Relationships matter: Linking teacher support to student engagement and achievement. *Journal of School Health, 74*(7), 262–273.

Kliebard, H. (1986). *The Struggle for the American Curriculum, 1893–1958*. New York: Routledge.

Koretz, D. (1992). *The Vermont Portfolio Assessment Program: Interim Report on Implementation and Impact, 1991–92 School Year*. Los Angeles, CA: National Center for Research on Evaluation, Standards, and Student Testing.

Koretz, D., Stecher, B., Klein, S., & McCaffrey, F. (1995). *The Vermont Portfolio Assessment Program: Findings and Implications*. Santa Monica, CA: RAND Corporation. www.rand.org/pubs/reprints/RP366.html

Ladson-Billings, G. (2014). Culturally relevant pedagogy 2.0: a.k.a. the remix. *Harvard Educational Review*, *84*(1), 74.

Lawrence Public Schools. (2017). *Welcome Back Letter to Parents Packet*. Accessed 11/1/18: www.lawrence.k12.ma.us/files/lps/LPSparentsguardians/Welcome_back_letter_to_parents_packet.pdf

Leithwood, K., & Louis, K. (Eds.). (1998). *Organizational Learning in Schools*. Abingdon, UK: Taylor & Francis.

Lorenz, E. N. (1963). Deterministic nonperiodic flow. *Journal of the Atmospheric Sciences*, *20*(2), 130–141. doi:10.1175/1520-0469(1963)020<0130:dnf>2.0.co;2

Lortie, D. (1975). *School Teacher: A Sociological Study*. Chicago: University of Chicago Press.

Lucey, T., Shifflet, R., & Weilbacher, G. (2014). Patterns of early childhood, elementary, and middle-level social studies teaching: An interpretation of Illinois social studies teachers' practices and beliefs. *The Social Studies*, *2014*(105), 283–290.

Mann, H. (1843). Mr. Mann's seventh annual report: Education in Europe. *The Common School Journal*, (6), 5–12, 84.

Marion, S. F., & Buckley, K. (2016). Design and implementation considerations of performance-based and authentic assessments for use in accountability systems. In H. Braun (Ed.), *Meeting the Challenges to Measurement in an Era of Accountability*. New York, NY: Routledge and Taylor & Francis, 2015.

Massachusetts Consortium for Innovative Education Assessment. www.mciea.org

McDonald, J., Mohr, N., Dichter, A., & McDonald, E. (2007). *The Power of Protocols: An Educator's Guide to Better Practice*. New York: Teachers College Press.

McGlynn, C. (2011). Negotiating difference in post-conflict Northern Ireland: An analysis of approaches to Integrated Education. *Multicultural Perspectives*, *13*(1), 16–22. doi:10.1080/15210960.2011.548179

McGuinn, P. (2006). *No Child Left behind and the Transformation of Federal Education Policy, 1965–2005*. Lawrence, KS: University of Kansas Press.

McLaughlin, M. (1990). The Rand change agent study revisited: Macro perspectives and micro realities. *Educational Researcher*, *19*(9), 11–16.

McMurrer, J. (2007). *Choices, Changes, and Challenges: Curriculum and Instruction in the NCLB Era*. Washington, DC: Center on Education Policy.

Meier, D. (1995). *The Power of Their Ideas: Lessons for America from a Small School in Harlem*. Boston: Beacon Press.

Miller, J., & Page, S. (2007). *Complex Adaptive Systems: An Introduction to Computational Models of Social Life*. Princeton, NJ: Princeton University Press.

Mintrop, H., & Sunderman, G. L. (2009). *Why High Stakes Accountability Sounds Good But Doesn't Work: And Why We Keep on Doing It Anyway*. Los Angeles, CA: The Civil Rights Project and Proyecto Derechos Civiles at UCLA. Accessed 2/22/19: www.civilrightsproject.ucla.edu

Moncada Linares, S. (2016). Othering: Towards a critical cultural awareness in the language classroom. *HOW*, *23*(1), 129–146. doi:10.19183/how.23.1.157

Moon, T., Brighton, C., Jarvis, J., & Hall, C. (2007). *State Standardized Testing Programs: Their Effects on Teachers and Students.* Storrs, CT: University of Connecticut and National Research Center on the Gifted and Talented.

Mourshed, M., Chijioke, C., & Barber, M. (2010). *How the World's Most Improved School Systems Keep Getting Better.* London: McKinsey & Company.

Murnane, R., & Levy, F. (1996). *Teaching the New Basic Skills: Principles for Educating Children to Thrive in a Changing Economy.* New York: Free Press.

Murnane, R., & Levy, F. (1997, February). A civil society demands education for good jobs. *Educational Leadership,* 34–36.

Murnane, R., Willett, J., & Levy, F. (1995). *The Growing Importance of Cognitive Skills in Wage Determination.* Working Paper No. 5076. Washington, DC: National Bureau of Economic Research, 15. doi:10.3386/w5076

The National Academies of Sciences, Engineering and Medicine. (2011). Defining deeper learning and 21st century skills. *Current Projects.* Division of Behavioral and Social Sciences and Education. www.nationalacademies.org/cp/committeeview

National Commission on Excellence in Education. (1983). *A Nation at Risk: The Imperative for Educational Reform: A Report to the Nation and the Secretary of Education.* Washington, DC: United States Department of Education.

National Research Council. (2012). *Education for Life and Work: Developing Transferable Knowledge and Skills in the 21st Century.* Committee on Defining Deeper Learning and 21st Century Skills, James W. Pellegrino and Margaret L. Hilton, Editors. Board on Testing and Assessment and Board on Science Education, Division of Behavioral and Social Sciences and Education. Washington, DC: The National Academies Press.

National School Reform Faculty. www.nsrfharmony.org; www.rightquestion.org

NBC Olympics. www.nbcolympics.com/news/diving-101-scoring

Nehring, J. (2009). *The Practice of School Reform: Lessons from Two Centuries.* Albany, NY: SUNY Press.

Nehring, J. (under review). *It Matters How You Manage Diversity: Cultural Difference in Northern Ireland's Secondary Schools.*

Nehring, J., Charner-Laird, M., & Szczesiul, S. (2017). What real high performance looks like. *Phi Delta Kappan,* 98(7), 38–42. doi:10.1177/0031721717702630

Nehring, J., Charner-Laird, M., & Szczesiul, S. (2019). Redefining excellence: Teaching in transition, from test performance to 21st century skills. *NASSP Bulletin,* 103(1), 1–27. doi:10.1177/0192636519830772

Nehring, J., & O'Brien, E. (2012). Strong gents and weak systems: University support for school level improvement. *Journal of Educational Change,* 13(4), 449–485. doi:10.1007/s10833-012-9187-0

Nehring, J., & Szczesiul, S. (2012). *How Four Educators Navigate the Twin Policy Demands for External Accountability and Twenty-First Century Knowledge: The United States Context.* Unpublished Manuscript.

Nehring, J., & Szczesiul, S. (2015). Redefining high performance in Northern Ireland: Deeper learning and 21st century skills meet high stakes accountability. *Journal of Educational Change,* 16(3), 327–348. doi:10.1007/s10833-015-9250-8

New Hampshire Department of Education. (2016). *Moving from Good to Great in New Hampshire: Performance Assessment of Competency Education (PACE)*. Concord, NH: New Hampshire Department of Education.

New York State Education Department. (2015, August 12). [Press Release] *State Education Department Releases Spring 2015 Grades 3–8 Assessment Results*. Albany, NY: Author. Accessed 2/22/19: www.nysed.gov/news/2015/state-education-department-releases-spring-2015-grades-3-8-assessment-results

Ogbu, J. U. (1978). *Minority Education and Caste: The American System in Cross-Cultural Perspective*. San Diego, CA: Academic Press.

Opposs, D. (2016). Whatever happened to school-based assessment in England's GCSEs and A-levels? *Perspectives in Education, 34*(4), 52–61. doi:10.18820/2519593X/pie.v34i4.4

Paris, D. (2012). Culturally sustaining pedagogy: A needed change in stance, terminology, and practice. *Educational Researcher, 41*(3), 93–97. doi:10.3102/0013189X12441244

Partnership for 21st Century Skills. (2003). *Learning for the 21st Century: A Report and Mile Guide for 21st Century Skills*. Partnership for 21st Century Skills. See Appendix A.

Pestalozzi, J. (1894). *How Gertrude Teaches Her Children* (L. E. Holland & F. C. Turner, Trans., E. Cooke, Ed., Intro. and Notes, p. xvi). Syracuse, NY: C.W. Bardeen. Accessed 2/22/19: https://archive.org/stream/howgertrudeteach00pestuoft/howgertrudeteach00pestuoft_djvu.txt

Pettigrew, T., & Tropp, L. (2006). A meta-analytic test of inter-group contact theory. *Journal of Personality and Social Psychology, 90*(5), 751–783. doi:10.1037/00223514.90.5.751

Ravitch, D. (2000). *The Death and Life of the Great American School System: How Testing and Choice Are Undermining Education*. New York: Basic Books.

Ravitch, D., & Finn, C. (1987). *What Do Our 17 Year Olds Know? A Report on the First National Assessment of History and Literature*. New York: HarperCollins.

Reese, W. (2001). The origins of progressive education. *History of Education Quarterly, 41*(1), 1–24.

Richardson, V., Anders, P., Tidwell, D., & Lloyd, C. (1991). The relationship between teachers' beliefs and practices in reading comprehension instruction. *American Educational Research Journal, 28*(3), 559–586.

Rothman, R., & Marion, S. F. (2016). The next generation of state assessment and accountability. *Kappan, 97*(8), 34–37.

Rousseau, J. (1921). *Emile, or Education* (M.A. Barbara Foxley, Trans.). London and Toronto: J.M. Dent & Sons; New York: E.P. Dutton. Accessed 10/12/2017: http://oll.libertyfund.org/titles/2256#Rousseau_1499_500, paragraph 500.

Rugg, H. (1937). *Man and His Changing Society*. Boston: Ginn and Company.

Rugg, H., Krueger, L., & Sondergaard, L. (1929). Studies in child personality: I. A study of the language of kindergarten children. *Journal of Educational Psychology, 20*(1), 1–18.

Saavedra, A. (2014). The academic impact of enrollment in International Baccalaureate Diploma Programs: A case study of Chicago Public Schools. *Teachers College Record, 4*(116), 6.

Saavedra, A. (2016). Academic civic mindedness and model citizenship in the International Baccalaureate Diploma Programme. *The Social Studies, 107*(1), 1–13.

Schleicher, A. (2015). *Schools for 21st-Century Learners: Strong Leaders, Confident Teachers, Innovative Approaches, International Summit on the Teaching Profession.* Paris: OECD Publishing.

School Reform Initiative. www.schoolreforminitiative.org

Scott, B. (2009). *Organization Development Primer: Change Management, Kurt Lewin and Beyond.* Belfast, Northern Ireland: Queens University.

Secretary's Commission on Achieving Necessary Skills. (1991). *What Work Requires of Schools: A SCANS Report for America 2000.* Washington, DC: United States Department of Labor.

Senge, P., Cambron-McCabe, N., Lucas, T., Smith, B., & Dutton, J. (2000). *Schools That Learn: A Fifth Discipline Fieldbook for Educators, Parents, and Everyone Who Cares About Education.* New York: Doubleday.

Shaw, L. (2006, November 5). Foundation's small schools experiment has yet to yield big results. *Seattle Times.* Accessed 11/1/18: www.seattletimes.com/seattle-news/foundations-small-schools-experiment-has-yet-to-yield-big-results/

Shulman, L. (1987). Knowledge and teaching: Foundations of the new reform. *Harvard Educational Review, 57*(1), 1–22.

Sizer, T. (1984). *Horace's Compromise: The Dilemma of the American High School.* Boston: Houghton Mifflin.

Smith, A. (2003, November). *Soul Wound: The Legacy of Native American Schools.* Amnesty Solution Tree. www.solutiontree.com

Sommeiller, E., & Price, M. (2018). The new gilded age: Income inequality in the U.S. by state, metropolitan area, and county. *Economic Policy Institute.* Accessed 2/22/19: www.epi.org

Stancil, W. (2018, March 14). School segregation is not a myth. *The Atlantic.* www.theatlantic.com/education/archive/2018/03/school-segregation-is-not-a-myth/555614/

Stepanek, J., Appel, G., Leong, M., Mangan, M., & Mitchell, M. (2007). *Leading Lesson Study: a Practical Guide for Teachers and Facilitators.* Thousand Oaks, CA: Corwin Press.

Suitts, S., Barba, P., & Dunn, K. (2015). *A New Majority: Low Income Students Now a Majority in the Nation's Public Schools.* Atlanta, GA: Southern Education Foundation. www.southerneducation.org/

Szczesiul, S., Nehring, J., & Carey, T. (2015). Academic task demand in the 21st-century, high-stakes-accountability school: Mapping the journey from poor [to fair to good to great] to excellent? *Leadership and Policy in Schools, 14*(4), 460–489. doi:10.1080/15700763.2015.1026448

Taylor, E., Gillborn, D., & Ladson-Billings, G. (2009). *Foundations of Critical Race Theory in Education.* New York: Routledge.

Thornton, S. J. (1991). Teacher as curricular-instructional gatekeeper in social studies. In J. P. Shaver (Ed.), *Handbook of Research on Social Studies Teaching and Learning* (pp. 237–248). New York: Macmillan Publishers.

Tyack, D., & Tobin, W. (1994). The "grammar" of schooling: Why has it been so hard to change? *American Educational Research Journal, 31*(3), 453–479.

United States Department of Education. (2001). *Reauthorization of the Elementary and Secondary Education Act: No Child Left Behind.* Title I, Part A, Section 1111, Subsections A and B. Accessed 1/9/18: www2.ed.gov/policy/elsec/leg/esea02/pg2.html#sec1111

United States Department of Education, Smaller Learning Communities Program. Accessed 11/1/18: www2.ed.gov/programs/slcp/funding.html

VanSledright, B., Maggioni, L., & Reddy, K. (2011, April). *Preparing Teachers to Teach Historical Thinking? The Interplay between Professional Development Programs and School-Systems' Cultures.* Paper presented at the 2011 annual meeting of the American Educational Research Association, New Orleans, LA.

Voice of San Diego. (2006, September 2). Questions for Larry Rosenstock. Accessed 1/11/18: www.voiceofsandiego.org/topics/news/questions-for-larry-rosenstock/

Voogt, J., & Roblin, N. (2012). A comparative analysis of international frameworks for 21st century competences: Implications for national curriculum policies. *Journal of Curriculum Studies, 44*(3), 299–321.

Wilder, T., Jacobsen, R., & Rothstein, R. (2008). *Grading Education: Getting Accountability Right.* New York: Teachers College Press, Economic Policy Institute, and Wiley.

Index

Note: Page numbers in bold indicate tables on the corresponding pages.